THE ONE MINUTE COACH

365 thought-provoking insights to start your day

JAEMIN FRAZER

THE ONE MINUTE COACH

2020 © by Jaemin Frazer.
All rights reserved. Printed in Australia.

No part of this book may be used or reproduced in any manner whatsoever without written permission except in the case of brief quotation embodied in critical articles and reviews.

For information contact the author at https://jaeminfrazer.com

National Library of Australia Cataloguing-in-Publication entry:

Frazer, Jaemin, author.

One Minute Coach

ISBN: 978-0-6488942-4-7 (hardcover)

Self Help

Mind Body

Foreword
by Katherine Frazer

I might sound biased, but this book is a favourite of mine. Jaemin had reached approximately 250 One Minute Coach radio segments when I said this would make a great book. It wasn't until someone else suggested it again twelve months later that Jaemin got on board with the idea (this has happened a number of times during the course of our marriage!) There's five years of Jaemin's blood, sweat and tears in here. And if only I had a dollar for every time he told me how hard it was to write a complete idea for one minute of airtime. Finally, he set about writing enough segments to have a thought for each day of the year.

For those of you that are new to the personal development space, and with the stigma of people not really understanding what life coaching is (lots of people in our hometown have no idea what he actually does) this book is a great introduction to improving the quality of your life.

You'll also be introduced to all the 'self-help' greats — Anthony Robbins, Tim Ferris, Stephen Covey, Seth Godin and Jordan Peterson — just to name a few; all the best they have to offer, as well as Jaemin's insights to live a full life unhindered by fear, doubt and limiting beliefs.

For someone who has been exposed to the personal development space like myself (it's a bit hard not to be when you're married to a life coach) I have found this book a wonderful reminder of lessons already learnt but can be applied to new situations and challenges. I have read this book many times already during the editing process over the last twelve months and, surprisingly, keep getting blown away at how a one-minute thought can be so relevant to a current situation, or a conversation I had just the other day.

The personal development journey is not one that will ever be fully completed in a lifetime. There is no end and once you've conquered one challenge a new one will arise. No challenges in your world right now? Then how are you planning for your future, growing your business, loving your spouse and kids, being grateful and living your best life?

This book is a game changer. Start your day with a thought-provoking insight. Ponder it for the rest of the day. Take 10 minutes to ask yourself some questions — how does this apply to my life right now? Journal your responses. Too much? Let it adorn your coffee table with its pretty cover. Gift it to your friends and family. It won't disappoint. (I already said I was biased!)

"This is, by far, the hardest thing I have ever done. To write a complete, clear, intelligent idea, that doesn't contradict or repeat another, written in half a page, recorded in one minute and does not just 'add to the noise.'"

— **Jaemin Frazer**

Contents

1. The illusion of no choice
2. Let go of blame and excuse
3. How is that working for you?
4. Train others how to treat you
5. The meaning we place on our experiences
6. Pick a better story
7. What do you want?
8. Well-formed outcomes
9. Self-protection signals
10. Outcome — intention — consequence
11. Manage your energy instead of your time
12. State is king
13. State management
14. Manage your state — Language
15. Manage your state — Focus
16. Manage your state — Physiology
17. Evidence for what we believe
18. The power of 'yet'
19. You are not your behaviour
20. Needs trump values
21. Willpower is a limited resource
22. Time and money are not as real as you think
23. Momentum = speed + weight + direction
24. Skillful manipulation
25. A big why
26. Priorities
27. Face up or run away
28. Pleasure and pain
29. The purpose of self-judgement
30. Chunk size
31. Proactive willpower
32. The gift of pain
33. Perfectionism is a lack of standards
34. Be-Do-Have
35. Self-talk programming
36. Morning rituals
37. Pick yourself
38. Resourceful certainty
39. Celebrate — Acknowledge — Reward
40. Values and rules
41. No behaviour management
42. Reframe safety
43. The danger of confidence
44. The power of focus
45. People work perfectly
46. The gift of doubt
47. Hurtfulness
48. Perception
49. Being too hasty
50. Busyness as an addiction
51. Course correction
52. Have to vs choose to
53. Frustration with others = frustration with self
54. The problem with positivity
55. Your body knows
56. Mindfulness — be external

57. Be the prize
58. Everything can be reframed
59. Quality questions
60. Smarter goals
61. Problem — Remedy — Outcome
62. Perceptual positions
63. Taking the handbrake off
64. Highest common agreement
65. Dispassionate observer
66. Ego and awareness cannot co-exist
67. Wanting
68. Negotiability
69. Fear is irrational
70. Emotional stability
71. Framing expectations
72. The importance of having bad days
73. The shadow effect
74. The body craves health
75. Anyone can be beautiful
76. Emotions
77. Success
78. Let go of unhappiness
79. Don't confuse simple with easy
80. Everything is created twice
81. Do you want to be well?
82. Getting back up again
83. Letting go of should
84. Humility
85. The power of visualisation
86. Social skills
87. The power of imagination
88. Coping with disappointment
89. Comparison
90. Winning is better than losing
91. The 4 A's of personal transformation
92. Unresourceful variety
93. Aligning head and heart
94. If you don't know what you want
95. Circle of control-influence-concern
96. Forgiveness
97. Letting go of labels
98. Ramsey-style honesty
99. The best way not to get hurt
100. The long haul
101. Be careful what you wish for
102. Set up a winning week
103. Meeting with yourself
104. Meeting with your stakeholders
105. Developing a rhythm of rest
106. Exercise and nutrition
107. Investing in key relationships
108. Daily rituals
109. Learning and development
110. Decisions
111. Who are you?
112. Language
113. The martyr syndrome
114. Laziness
115. The fear of success — Part 1
116. The fear of success — Part 2
117. The fear of success — Part 3
118. The fear of success — Part 4
119. The fear of success — Part 5
120. Letting go of the can
121. Real generosity
122. Secrets to great relationships
123. Speaking into someone else's reality
124. Hope is not a plan and sorry is not a solution
125. Overcomplicating issues
126. Navigating past gatekeepers
127. Stress
128. Energy and rest
129. Be happy and significant
130. Modelling success
131. Overthinking
132. Accountability
133. Nuance
134. Building trust
135. The power of 'this'
136. Story
137. Narcissism is never narcissism
138. Peace comes from resolution
139. The game isn't over until you give up
140. Front foot or back foot living
141. Top five happiness tips
142. The power of metaphors
143. Shiny object syndrome

144. Influencing others
145. Proving your worth
146. Friendships
147. Learning to fight well
148. The clouded mind
149. Bright spots
150. To sell is human
151. Just take action
152. Flow state
153. Parkinson's Law
154. Applaud failure
155. Are you lying to yourself?
156. The importance of desire
157. Joy
158. Find your gold
159. Success is a science
160. Courage
161. Go where the life is
162. Ego
163. Spiral Dynamics
164. Moving beyond survival
165. Moving beyond tribe
166. Moving beyond rebellion
167. Moving beyond the system
168. Moving beyond entrepreneurship
169. Moving beyond contribution
170. Growth through experience
171. Dirty emotions
172. Decluttering
173. Gratitude in advance
174. The curse of knowledge
175. High and low-quality problems
176. Life is not fair
177. Romance
178. Parents
179. Energy
180. The Karpman Drama Triangle
181. All alone in the world
182. Get your power back
183. Listen to your dreams
184. Less hustle. More flow and ease
185. Stop and breathe
186. You are stronger than you think
187. Multitasking misconception
188. The illusion of safety
189. You've changed
190. Self-acceptance
191. Be anyone you want
192. Submitting to a teacher
193. Peak performance
194. Letting go
195. Illusions
196. The right framework
197. How does change happen?
198. Resisting change
199. What you seek is seeking you
200. Pretending not to know
201. Finding your purpose in life
202. Keep learning and growing
203. To say yes means also saying no
204. Every thought strengthens or weakens you
205. Create a life you don't need an escape from
206. Self-sabotage
207. Overcoming self-sabotage
208. Winning lotto
209. Relationship rules
210. Power and grace
211. Get a new jumper
212. Five big mistakes
213. Three keys for lasting change
214. State is king — Part 2
215. How is this not a problem?
216. The parable of the talents
217. Blame
218. Don't attach yourself to one vehicle
219. Are you ready for what you want?
220. Giving advice
221. Failing at what you don't want
222. How to give an effective apology
223. Choose the path with the best story
224. The opposite of depression
225. No guarantees
226. The issue is never the issue
227. Ask how can I, not just can I
228. Madness
229. Five steps to increasing productivity

230. What to do when things are hard — Part 1
231. What to do when things are hard — Part 2
232. Dealing with self-doubt
233. How well do you apologise?
234. The dragon in the cave
235. Removing other options
236. Get over yourself
237. Measuring success
238. When you're not sure what to do
239. You need a lot less than you think you do
240. Adding to the noise
241. Don't lose sight of what you want — Part 1
242. Don't lose sight of what you want — Part 2
243. Insecurity will cost you
244. The best of you behaving badly
245. Judging others
246. Time — money — mobility
247. Jump off the merry-go-round
248. Who do you say you are?
249. Twelve signs of insecurity
250. Limiting beliefs have a payoff
251. Complaining is madness
252. What are you keeping track of?
253. Courage over confidence
254. Uncomfortable conversations
255. Rest
256. Don't make decisions out of fear
257. It is what it is
258. Optimising happiness
259. Keep growing
260. My top three personal development tips
261. The power of being relaxed
262. Love and fear
263. Living between on and off
264. Raising confident children
265. A believable plan
266. Goal setting
267. Happiness is found in solving problems
268. Story — state — strategy
269. Honour the gift
270. Women and personal development
271. Men and personal development
272. Dealing with shame
273. Real hope vs false hope
274. Endless possibilities
275. Seasons of relationships
276. Back down when you're wrong
277. Rome wasn't built in a day
278. Handling disappointment
279. The importance of being wrong
280. Dealing with narcissists
281. The fine trap
282. How to handle pressure
283. Letting go of lack
284. Different forms of happiness
285. Weak vs strong surrender
286. Powerful presupposition — Part 1
287. Powerful presupposition — Part 2
288. The power of being vulnerable
289. Self-permission
290. The five guiding principles of highly successful people
291. Anxiety
292. Be here now
293. Problems
294. How to be a pessimist
295. How to be an optimist
296. Yes and no
297. Just like me?
298. Your part in the mess
299. Breaking the cycle of cause and effect
300. The importance of embracing the dark side
301. Seeking validation
302. People have done more with less
303. Setbacks
304. Busyness = laziness and laziness = fear
305. Craving certainty
306. The difference between blame and responsibility
307. Your job is supposed to suck

308. Why people don't listen to their pain
309. Life is suffering
310. Nesting in your hair
311. Productivity
312. Change is hard
313. One-minute manager
314. Self-deception
315. Purpose
316. Fully becoming an adult
317. Go back before moving forward
318. Reviewing your story
319. Freedom poem
320. The adult question
321. Reconciling disappointment
322. Internal representation
323. Be impeccable with your word
324. Less to more
325. Start with who
326. What is wisdom?
327. Getting your MEDS right
328. Thinking new thoughts
329. Changing your partner
330. Dress like today is important
331. Review your agreements
332. Set clear intentions
333. Problem-solving questions
334. Review questions
335. You are not the victim. You are the persecutor
336. The subject-object switch
337. What is your quest?
338. Out of fear and into process
339. Practice 1 — Step into the light
340. Practice 2 — Take 100% responsibility
341. Practice 3 — Stack the pain
342. Practice 4 — Develop a compelling life vision
343. Practice 5 — Get help from someone who doesn't care about you
344. Practice 6 — Be the hero
345. Practice 7 — Re-write the story
346. Mistake 1 — Running away from the fear
347. Mistake 2 — Hoping to be rescued
348. Mistake 3 — Using pain against yourself
349. Mistake 4 — Dreaming in the dark
350. Mistake 5 — Getting help from the wrong people
351. Mistake 6 — Fighting the wrong battle
352. Mistake 7 — Rushing to the end too soon
353. Self-sabotage
354. Let go of the illusion it could've been different
355. Gratitude — progress — optimism
356. The sunk cost bias
357. Having a clear rationale
358. Moving from the known to the unknown
359. Abundance vs scarcity
360. Worrying about the future
361. Live as though your father is dead
362. Assertiveness is fruit
363. Gaslighting
364. Deep change
365. Subtracting

1
The Illusion of No Choice

As a life coach, one of the most common challenges I see people bring to the table is a sense of hopelessness.

For some people, nothing is working and they feel completely hopeless. Or sometimes it's just one thing in their life that feels hopeless. Perhaps their business is going great, but they have no idea how to talk to their 14-year-old son. Or maybe their finances are great, yet their health problems are causing a lot of suffering.

Hope is linked to choice. The root of hopelessness is feeling that you have no choice. If you have five options and four fail, there is still hope. But if all five don't work out, hope evaporates.

One of the most amazing things to discover is that this feeling of having no choice is simply an illusion. The illusion of no choice. In fact, we each have 100% choice over the things that really matter in life and are therefore exactly where we have chosen to be. Sure, we might not choose what happens to us, but we always get to choose our response. The moment we embrace choice, hope returns.

2
Let Go of Blame and Excuse

The two things that amaze me most in life are firstly, how extraordinarily powerful we are as human beings, and secondly, how much power most people give away to live as disempowered victims.

We are each capable of so much, yet many people live as though they are incapable and broken, waiting for someone or something to turn their life around for them. I'm amazed at people's capacity to just get by and survive. All the while complaining about their lot in life but never doing anything to change it.

The issue, as Spiderman says, is that with great power comes great responsibility[1]. The reason power is given away so frequently is because people opt for the safe approach.

If you give away your power when things go bad, it's not your responsibility and therefore, never your fault. While that may protect you from failure, unfortunately all that leaves you with is blame and excuse.

Success in any area starts when we realise that our results are exactly that — our results. We get the chance to improve our results only by letting go of blame and excuse and taking 100% responsibility.

3
How is that Working for You?

So often, the stuff happening in people's lives isn't what they'd like it to be. Yet, the reality is every negative thing in our lives that we complain about, or even tolerate, must be giving us some kind of payoff or reward.

It was Dr Phil[2] who first popularised this basic aspect of human behavioural science.

When someone comes on his show complaining about how bad their life is, his classic response is to ask, 'So how is that working for you?'

'It's not,' they say. 'Weren't you listening? Let me tell you again how unfair and horrible it is.'

'Well, clearly it's working, otherwise you wouldn't still be doing it.'

In truth, we are actually not silly enough to continue with behaviour if it's not giving us anything in return. We may do something once for no reward, but not twice, and definitely not for weeks, months or years.

The payoff for tolerating negative stuff is always along the lines of self-protection, comfort, comparison and pity. It all feeds into our ego and meets our core needs. One of the most important aspect of lasting change, therefore, is to be willing to let go of the payoff for staying the same.

4
Train Others How to Treat You

I often hear people complain about how badly others treat them.

One of my very first coaching clients told me she'd only been happy for the first six weeks of her 30-year marriage. She complained her husband was 'large and in charge' and controlled everything about their relationship. On top of all of this, he didn't even know she was unhappy. She suffered in silence, desperate to know when he would change and love her like she deserved.

But why in the world would he change? He had zero motivation to do anything different simply because he already had everything working in his favour. I'm not justifying his behaviour, but if she wanted him to change, she'd need to stop blaming him and start taking responsibility for training him to treat her like that for 30 years.

See — we are each 100% responsible for training others how to treat us by what we allow and what we deny. My client had taught her husband he could have his cake AND eat it, and he obliged.

Blame is natural, but it gives all your power away to the other person so you have no ability to change anything. Taking 100% responsibility, on the other hand, means you have the power to bring about change.

5
The Meaning We Place on Our Experiences

I work with a lot of people who have suffered abuse of some kind in their past. It is common for these people to feel their life is messed up because of what has happened to them. Without diminishing the horrible nature of abuse, the reality is that it was not the abuse that ruined their life, but instead the meaning they gave to the event and the story they told themselves about why they were abused.

The quality of our life is not shaped by the things that happen to us, but entirely by the meaning we place on these things. We are sense-making creatures and as such, have to give meaning to every event, conversation and experience throughout our entire life. Two people can go through exactly the same experience and come out the other side with two totally different meanings.

Typically, when bad things happen to us, however, we seem to choose a negative meaning, pointing the blame at ourselves. If you want to flourish in life, it is crucial to keep picking meanings that serve you. The great news is, that even when you've chosen a meaning in the past that has diminished you, it's always possible to go back, decide you were wrong and choose a better meaning.

6
Pick a Better Story

I'm always fascinated by the key differences between those who struggle and those who flourish when it comes to their approach to life. It turns out that those who succeed in any area of life are not necessarily the people with the most skill, talent or giftedness.

There are plenty of people who've had everything going for them and seemed certain to succeed, yet never did. Then there are those who seemed to have no right to succeed and nothing going for them, yet still found a way.

Much of this success comes down to the stories they live out of. The stories they tell others about who they are, what they are capable of, where they belong and what they deserve. Now, we don't actually get to see reality, just our perception of reality. So really, it's all just stories.

People who succeed just tell better stories than those who don't. What's more, they realise that they are just stories and so they change the story when it stops working for them.

How are your stories working for you? Maybe it's time to pick a better story.

7
What Do You Want?

I was running a coaching workshop for some year 11 students recently and asked the most basic coaching questions: What do you want? What's the dream? What are the goals for your future? Amazingly, very few of them had an answer. The funny thing is that I'd only spoken to a group of year 3 kids a week earlier, asking them the same question and everybody knew!

What could have changed in a young person's life in such a short time? Sadly, the answer is that they've already worked out in their mind that's not how life works. You don't get what you want. You make do with your lot in life. You take your cues from what those around you are doing and settle and survive instead. They have seen that to ask yourself what you want is a dangerous question as it opens up the potential for failure and disappointment.

Although they are correct in their observation of the potential dangers, we are designed to flourish not just survive. To desire is human. If you shut this down, it is like putting your humanity on hold.

Success starts by giving yourself permission to ask these dangerous but beautifully important questions. It is essential to be clear about what you are looking for in every area of life.

8
Well-formed Outcomes

Doing life well starts with having a clear sense of what you're actually aiming for. Most people get the fact that goal setting is important, yet the way they go about it often makes it impossible to achieve.

When people first explore what they want, they often state it in big, broad abstract language, "I want to be fit…I want to be happy…I want to have financial freedom…I want a great marriage…I want to be a great mum."

The problem with these kinds of goals is that they are not actually goals at all and, therefore, can never be achieved. It may sound like you've been clear, but in fact you haven't said anything. Using grand abstract language to describe what you want is the best way to guarantee you'll never achieve it.

What is fit? How would you know you're fit? Fit by who's standard? When do you want this fitness by?

The key is to have well-formed outcomes. This means creating structure and substance within the goal itself. Unless you can measure it, you can't have it.

9
Self-protection Signals

One of the cool things about being human is that we have an inbuilt system for self-protection and avoiding danger. Therefore, when you stumble upon a potentially hazardous situation in life, your subconscious will give you all kinds of signals to tell you that you're in danger and to try and protect you.

What usually happens is that we consciously suppress or turn off these signals because we believe we can't afford to listen to them. There are a bunch of external pressures and expectations to meet, which makes it inconvenient to heed our own warning signals.

The problem is, that if you keep suppressing all the natural signals and forge on regardless, you can create such internal discord that the subconscious screams 'this is not sustainable' and throws up massive anxiety, chronic fatigue, depression, injury or illness to get you out of the situation. Ultimately, this eventually leads to trauma, which is where your relationship with yourself is broken altogether.

People who do life really well, on the other hand, actually work with themselves not against themselves. This starts and ends by building rapport with their own being and learning to trust their internal signals.

10
Outcome – Intention – Consequence

Doing life well certainly starts with being very clear about the kind of life you desire to live, and how you define success in the first place. It's essential to have well-formed outcomes for your life.

Dr Ian Snape from The Coaching Space taught me a fantastic Neuro Linguistic Programming (NLP) model to do this well. It's called: outcome, intention, consequence.[3]

Here is how it works:

a) Outcome. What do I want? What would I like to have happen?

b) Intention. If I had that, what would that give me? What is the intention behind the outcome? You actually don't want the 'thing', it's what the thing represents that's really appealing.

c) Consequence. What are the consequences of getting these outcomes? List all the upsides and downsides. Everything comes with a price.

Once you have had a look at these three areas is there anything you'd like to change?

Imagine taking this model to the big line outside the newsagent next time Powerball is at $40 million. Sure, the people in the line know what they want, but I could almost guarantee they haven't explored why they want it and the costs of actually getting it.

11
Manage Your Energy Instead of Your Time

People who succeed in life realise it is far more important to manage their energy rather than their time.

It turns out that energy is a far more useful resource than time could ever be. If you have two days to get an important task done but you're in a poor state and have no energy, all that time is almost useless to you. Yet, if you're in the zone and your energy levels are peaking, what you can accomplish in just one hour is extraordinary.

True peak performance in any arena is never an issue of time management. Success doesn't come by trying to squeeze more stuff into the day, but by learning how to bring your best to the table in the moments that matter most. If you manage your energy, your time will take care of itself.

The key question then becomes, what gives you energy and what takes your energy away? Your best use of time then becomes to manage your energy. For example, taking a 90-minute nap after lunch may result in a dynamic 30-minute burst of creative energy when you return to work. Although this seems counter-intuitive, your best results are always achieved when you have the most energy.

12
State is King

We all have incredible potential inside us, and we all have moments of brilliance, but the real question is: can you access the best of you when the game is on the line? Learning to manage your state means you can access the magic when you need it most.

It's a myth to believe that hard work is the only missing ingredient between you and your goals. I'm sure you've seen people work harder and harder to achieve things that always seem just out of their reach. Perhaps this is your experience of life right now.

It turns out that the key question is not what do I need to do, but who do I need to BE? Your state of being is the biggest thing affecting the outcomes you're getting right now. If you can control your state, you can control your outcomes.

It's what separates the top sports stars from those who never quite make it. The top 100 athletes in any sport would all have very similar skill levels. Yet when the pressure is on and the game is on the line, the winners are not determined by skill level but by who can control their state and, therefore, can access the magic when they need it most.

State is king. The top performers in any arena are not necessarily the strongest, smartest or most gifted but, without exception, they're the best at managing their state.

13
State Management

There are three basic components that make up every emotional state in which you find yourself. Your language, focus and physiology come together to determine your state. Therefore, if you change any of these three things, your state automatically changes as well.

Notice how slight changes to the words you use, what you are doing with your body, and where you are focusing your attention affect your state.

When people come to me in a poor state, feeling frustrated, angry or anxious, they often complain they have no control over their state and certainly didn't choose to feel like this. However, this is an example of the illusion of no choice. While it is true, they may not have chosen that end result, they have chosen the language, focus and physiology that has produced the emotional state they now find themselves in.

Learning to be mindful of these three things then becomes a crucial aspect of controlling your state

14
Manage Your State – Language

One of the simplest ways to manage your state is to change your language.

The words we use don't just describe how we feel — they shape our feelings and create our experience of life. Therefore, if you change the words you use, you also change the experience you have.

I used to describe myself as a big risk taker, but have since discovered this creates a high anxiety state where I feel like there is so much pressure and I could lose everything. So, I changed the language and started calling myself an adventurer instead.

Changing that one word has given me a totally different experience of my reality. As an adventurer, I look forward to challenges and problem solving. I want to take the path that will result in the best story to tell afterwards.

My kids aren't allowed to say they hate broccoli. It's not that 'hate' is a dirty word — it's just a word that will make them vomit when I put broccoli on their plate.

Notice the words you are using to shape your reality at the moment and see what happens to your state when you change them.

State is king. When you change your language, your state changes too.

15
Manage Your State – Focus

Another way to manage your energy and your state is to change what you are focusing your attention on.

We have so much choice in life, yet focus is one of the key choices we are often oblivious to in any moment. The reality is, we can't focus on everything. We just don't have the capacity to take everything in at the same time. However, what you do choose to focus on massively affects your state.

People who do life well, focus on things that give them more life and energy and create a great state, while those who live unhappy lives pay attention to very different things.

You can focus on the opportunities or the problems, the upside or the downside, the costs or the benefits, the pleasure or the pain, the people who like you or hate you, the things you are good at or the things you are bad at, the past or future.

You get the point. What you focus on becomes more prominent in your life and totally shapes how you feel.

State is king. When you change your focus, you also change your state.

16
Manage Your State – Physiology

Language and focus can change your state, but another great way to shift how you're feeling is to adjust your physiology. What we do with our body totally affects our mood. Diet, sleep, exercise, breathing, music, clothing, hair and makeup, stretching and body posture all play massive roles in our state, both positively and negatively.

For example, if you want to feel depressed, one of the quickest ways into that state is to lead with your physiology. If you were to sit down, drop your head into your hands and rub your face while sighing deeply, your state would instantly change. Suddenly, your mind would be bombarded with thoughts of past regrets, failures and all the things that are not going well for you right now. Next, you'll find yourself flooded with a bunch of negative emotions, leaving you feeling flat and sad. You are well on your way to becoming very depressed.

On the other hand, it would be very hard to feel depressed while you're dancing around the lounge room in your socks and undies, belting out your favourite song with the sun streaming through the window and the scent of freshly-brewed coffee in the air.

State is king. Change what you do with your body and you change your state.

17
Evidence for What We Believe

The brain has an amazing filter system. Every second of the day we are being bombarded with over 2 million pieces of information. We couldn't even try to be present to every one of these. In fact, we can only be aware of around seven pieces of information at a time, so our brain is constantly making lightning decisions about what to filter in or out.

The vast majority of the stuff available to our senses gets deleted while our brain generalises and distorts the rest to fit our belief system of what we expect to find in the world.

It turns out that having evidence that something is true is often highly unreliable and subjective. Why? Because our brain will find evidence for whatever we believe.

Life then becomes somewhat like a self-fulfilling prophecy. If you believe that everyone likes you, that's what you seem to discover in the world. Likewise, if you believe no one really likes you, even when people genuinely do, your brain distorts the evidence to prove you're right.

My point here is not to try and unsettle your concrete notion of reality, but to give you more choice so that you are able to change any negative patterns you'd like to be free from and to create a story that works well for you.

18
The Power of 'Yet'

I love the fact that great coaching is really just about giving people more choice.

Often people get stuck with the illusion of no choice and, as a result, feel really hopeless. Making great choices doesn't have to be about massive changes. Sometimes the choice to do one small thing differently can bring about some significant change.

I love the power of language — not just to describe how we feel but also to shape our experience. The moment you change your language, you ultimately change your experience.

One of my favourite small changes to language is adding the word 'yet' at the end of a sentence. One little word has the power to change how you feel about your current reality.

I can't work out how to do this...yet.

I haven't experienced the kind of success in my business I was hoping for...yet.

I don't have a great relationship with my boss...yet.

I don't like brussel sprouts...yet.

Add this little word to your life and see what it opens up for you.

19
You are Not Your Behaviour

One of Anthony Robbins' finest contributions to the realm of human behavioural science is his work on six core needs[4]. His theory is that everyone has the need for certainty, variety, significance, love, contribution and growth.

These needs will be filled in our lives no matter what. We can either have high-quality, resourceful ways of meeting them or low-quality unresourceful ways that end up hurting us, and others. This means that every single behaviour is in some way an attempt to fill a need, whether we are aware of it or not.

Often, we are quick to label ourselves, and each other, by our behaviour. But when we let go of the judgement, however, this model helps us to see that we are not our behaviour. Every behaviour is simply an attempt to meet one or more of our core needs.

One of the most crucial elements to doing life well is to separate behaviour from intention. This helps us to see the 'why' behind the 'what', and to keep finding high quality ways of meeting our needs in line with our values so we can let go of problem behaviour.

20
Needs Trump Values

Separating behaviour from intention, by understanding the need that it's meeting, enables us to let go of the self-judgement and find better ways to meet our needs.

One of the key thoughts in Anthony Robbins six core needs model is that 'needs override values'. This explains why good people do bad things. Why people who value honesty, lie; why people who value health, smoke or overeat; why people who value integrity, cheat.

Every negative behaviour has a positive intention. We are, in some way, trying to bring peace and comfort to ourselves. We don't do bad things because we are bad people. We do bad things because we are needy people and haven't found a better way to meet that need.

The path to growth and change always begins with awareness. If you can't see it, you can't change it. Take a step back and re-evaluate the behaviour you're trying to change in your life by exploring the need it's filling.

21
Willpower is a Limited Resource

One of the most common, and also most unhelpful, myths about success is that it's totally connected to how hard you're prepared to work. The constant advice is always to try harder, be better, be more disciplined, have more energy, stay focused, be committed, stay driven and maintain passion.

Yet willpower as a panacea is massively overrated. Willpower is like a muscle. It gets tired and runs out. People often use it as a behaviour management tool to cover up the bad fruit their life is producing, rather than actually deal with the root cause of the problem. Some seem to have more willpower than others, yet at some point, it will inevitably run out.

Willpower, when used well, is incredibly effective, yet your will is only one player in the context of the whole team of players that make up you as a person. Willpower is only one aspect of the self-improvement process. The key to get the best results is to use it in conjunction with your emotions, intuition and environment as part of a holistic change strategy.

22
Time and Money are Not as Real as You Think

I'll guarantee that successful people tell their stories about time and money differently from people who experience a lack in both these areas.

To most people, time and money seem like concrete realities that they're always working against. Yet amazingly, time and money are incredibly flexible. Both are a construct of the mind and, therefore, you can change your relationship with them.

Five minutes is experienced totally differently if you have to hold on for an available toilet as opposed to saying goodbye to a loved one heading overseas. Likewise, the last 10 years feels like a different length of time than thinking about the 10 years in front of you.

If you're sitting at a table with 10 people and they all pull $50 from their pocket, it may look as though there are 10 identical items on the table, but every note is actually different. Each person's note captures a range of different desires, expectations and fears based on what's happening in their world and their relationship with money.

It turns out that time and money take on the qualities and characteristics we bring to them rather than the other way around. This means each of us has the opportunity to change our relationship with time and money as we grow as human beings.

23
Momentum = Speed + Weight + Direction

Psychological studies show that there is a clear link between happiness and progress. Whenever we go around in circles or bang our head on the same brick wall, it totally affects our sense of personal wellbeing.

In order to make progress in life, you need momentum, which, if you remember from school, is the measure of how hard it is to stop an object in motion. It's the combination of speed + weight + direction.

To be happy, you have to make progress. To make progress, you need momentum. This means you will need to have increasing amounts of speed and weight in a specified direction.

Now stay with me here, because I'm not suggesting you get out your running shoes and eat lots of cheeseburgers. To break through the metaphor, having speed in life is all about action, passion, energy, drive, commitment and resilience. To add weight means acquiring knowledge, skills, experience, character and wisdom. And finally, you need to set a clear direction that is in line with your most important values, desires and goals.

24
Skilful Manipulation

John Maxwell says leadership can simply be summed up as influence: 'Leadership is influence. Nothing more nothing less.'[5] Therefore, great leaders exert a positive influence on others to do more than they would have done without this leadership.

Some time ago, I was coaching a guy who was trying to bring some positive change within his family, and he said, 'but I just don't want to manipulate my wife!' To his great surprise, I told him that was exactly what he needed to do.

See we all know a dodgy salesperson who's given manipulation a bad name, but the word actually means, 'to handle skilfully'. To manipulate others for your own selfish agenda is horrible, but to handle them skilfully to help them get a great result is really cool.

Great marriages, teams, businesses and families are built on people bringing their best to the game and not being afraid to skilfully handle each other rather than being afraid of manipulation.

Influence always requires manipulation.

25
A Big Why

Asking high-quality questions allows us to discover more effective and creative answers. Examining the words how and why gives us an example of the impact two questions of different quality can have on our lives.

Asking How? is typically a low-quality question. It's also the slowest way to solve any problem. How am I going to find a way? How do I earn more money? How do I improve my relationships?

The problem with how is that it searches back through your life, looking for historical evidence for how you've done it in the past. If you've never done it before, the answer comes back as 'I don't know how', which makes the way forward seem impossible! It is common to get paralysed in the how.

The better question is: Why? Why is this important? Why must I find a way?

When the why becomes big enough, the how takes care of itself. Every cool thing in life was at some point impossible. Remember, necessity is the mother of all invention!

Stop asking how and stay focused on why and you'll create a way that has never existed before.

26
Priorities

Stephen Covey's book, The 7 Habits of Highly Effective People, contributes so much to the idea of living life well. Covey suggests that people who succeed in life are guided by the compass, not the clock.

This means that instead of starting each day by focusing on a 'to-do list' in order to maximise your time, Covey says we should begin by focusing on our purpose in life and the values that are most important about the kind of life we want to lead.

This is being purpose driven and ordering your life from the top down, rather than starting with the urgent demands of the tasks in front of you and then trying to live out your values in your spare time. Once you are clear on the things that are most important to you, knowing how to use your time is so much easier.

If what seems urgent always gets your attention, sooner or later the time for the meaningful things evaporates altogether. This is important — don't wait until it's too late to find this out!

27
Face Up or Run Away

....

To do life well, it is essential to have healthy self-esteem. Nathaniel Branden's book The Psychology of Self-Esteem, shows us how that is possible.

Life happens. Each new day presents new problems, challenges and opportunities. We then have a choice to face up or run away from the reality of our life.

We can own, accept, confront and take responsibility. Or we can hide, blame, avoid and pretend. If we run away, we get shame, guilt and anxiety. If we face up, we get strength, confidence and peace.

Every time we run, we teach ourselves that we can't. The lesson to ourselves is that we don't have what it takes and need to keep running. Facing up, on the other hand, teaches us that we can. We come out the other side seeing that we have what it takes to deal with life.

Running ends up creating a limiting belief that you are no good or not enough. Facing up leads us to believe we are worthy and enough.

One path leads to poor self-esteem. The other leads to healthy self-esteem. So here is the question: Do you want to feel good about yourself? Face up to life. Every time you run away, you undermine your self-esteem.

28
Pleasure and Pain

The two greatest motivators in life are the pursuit of pleasure and the avoidance of pain. Everything we do in life is, in some way, driven by these two things. There is always a measure of both pleasure and pain in everything we do but depending on which one is greater will determine our behaviour.

One of the best ways to bring about change in your life, therefore, is to adjust your pleasure and pain associations. This is why the government have put grotesque images on cigarette packaging in an attempt to stop people smoking. They are trying to link it with pain rather than pleasure. However, this strategy is largely ineffective because 'pleasure and pain' is all about focus, and it is possible for smokers to simply ignore the packet and focus on the enjoyment they get instead.

Pleasure and pain associations are actually changed when someone stacks the pain on what they want to stop and builds pleasure towards what they want to start instead.

One of the best ways to do this is by focusing on the costs and rewards both now and into your future.

As soon as you link enough pain and pleasure to the right things, every cell in your body starts naturally helping the change process rather than resisting it.

29
The Purpose of Self-Judgement

One of the heaviest, most unproductive things we carry in life is self-judgement. People are so much harder on themselves than anyone else. Yet self-judgement has a positive intention and, contrary to popular opinion, it's not to try and make you a better, stronger person.

It's actually a pre-emptive strike. We fear the judgement of others, so we get in first and beat ourselves down so that if, and when, others do it, it doesn't hurt as much. Therefore, self-judgement is actually all about self-protection. So what about the purpose of protection?

What's really cool is that we only protect that which we deeply value. Therefore, self-protection is an honest form of self-love. Self-judgement is all about trying to love yourself.

We protect ourselves from failure, disappointment and being hurt by others, by hurting ourselves first! This is because we love ourselves and not because we think we are worthless. Knowing that it's true, I bet there is a better way of loving yourself than being so self-critical!

30
Chunk Size

One of the cool coaching terms to help us improve the way we process all the information available to us is 'chunking'. Chunking is about grouping individual bits of information together so they're easier to manage. For example, your phone number is chunked into three groups of three or four numbers to make it easier to remember.

Anthony Robbins explains that sometimes people feel overwhelmed because the chunk size they are using is too big or too small for their mind to cope with.[6]

For example, you might feel overwhelmed because 'everything' is going wrong for you. This means you're operating with one giant chunk of information. To bring the chunk size down, ask yourself: What specifically is going wrong? It may mean you end up with just three key areas to work on instead of one massive one.

Alternatively, you may feel stressed because you have a 'thousand' things to do. This means the chunk size is now too small. You could chunk up by grouping your task list into three categories or exploring the purpose of why you're doing these things in the first place.

This changes the size and complexity of the chunks you're dealing with, which also totally changes how overwhelmed you may feel.

31
Proactive Willpower

Willpower is a limited resource and, just like a muscle, it gets tired. Most people place far too much dependence on their own ability to discipline themselves and wonder why they find themselves rarely making long-term progress. However, if you are going to utilise the strength of this muscle, here are three keys to get the most out of your willpower.

1. Don't waste your willpower with decision fatigue. If you give yourself too many options about what you could do to get the desired result, you'll waste all your energy trying to work out which path is best and then be too tired to do anything about it. Pick one or two things and just go with it.

2. Be proactive. Use your willpower ahead of time, not in the moment. Let's say you want to exercise more. Studies show that if you make the key decisions about route, distance, food, shoes etc. the night before, you are much more likely to carry out the plan the next day. When the alarm goes off in the morning at joke o'clock, all you need your willpower to do is execute the plan and get you out the door. There's no need to stuff around making decisions about the route and distance while trying to remember where you put your stupid shoes.

3. Use this muscle in conjunction with the range of other forms of internal motivation. Willpower is just one of the resources available to motivate you. It's certainly not the only tool for getting the best out of yourself.

32
The Gift of Pain

If you're not accustomed to listening to yourself, the best place to start is with pain. Pain is your most honest voice to yourself. When you're not fighting against yourself, you can actually stop and listen to what's going on inside. See pain as a gift.

I was reading a story recently about a 5-year-old leprosy sufferer who bit the end off her finger and wrote her name on her bedroom wall in blood — because she could. This disease attacks the nervous system, which means pain signals stop entirely. If you put your hand in fire, it's actually supposed to hurt so that you quickly remove your hand before it gets badly burnt.

Yet, in today's world, we often treat pain as a bad thing. We mask, medicate and avoid pain wherever possible.

Pain is designed to protect us from further pain. If you ignore it, then there is nothing to stop you destroying your own life, just as surely as you will get burnt if you touch the fire.

The main reason people don't listen to pain is that they think it will require them to change something hard. However, suppressing emotional, mental and physical pain will always cost you more in the long run.

33
Perfectionism is a Lack of Standards

A common misconception when it comes to peak performance is that you need to be a perfectionist to succeed. This couldn't be further from the truth. Perfectionism can be defined as having a lack of standards. It is easy to think perfectionists have incredibly high standards, yet upon closer inspection, it becomes apparent that they have no standards at all.

Someone who has perfectionist behaviour has never actually decided what standard they're reaching for. All they are aware of is that their current performance is not good enough: The house is not clean enough, the assignment hasn't been written well enough, they haven't spent enough time with the kids, or they haven't worked hard enough.

The only time they stop doing a task is when an external deadline forces them to. This all stems from a limiting belief about not being good enough.

The key is not to deal with the behaviour, but the underlying belief. Until a person realises that they are enough, and that 'perfect' is an artificial and unachievable distinction, they will keep driving themselves too hard.

Believing that you're a good person and that you're enough, means there's nothing to prove and you can set appropriate standards and no longer try to be a perfectionist.

34
BE – DO – HAVE

There are three common approaches to trying to get ahead in life — the Victim, the Worker and the Winner.

The Victim orients their life this way: HAVE — DO — BE.

When I HAVE enough time, money and support, then I'll DO the things I've always wanted to, and then I'll BE happy and successful. The problem is they don't HAVE. So they are always waiting for externals to change, and comparing themselves to those who already have all the things they need.

The Worker positions themselves like this: DO — HAVE — BE. The more I DO, the more I'll HAVE, the happier I'll BE. The problem is that the more they DO, the more there is still to do. They get defined by what they do and become driven, busy and tired. Additionally, the more they HAVE, the more there is to have and now the more there is to lose. Being happy is constantly out of their reach and so never arrives.

The Winner, on the other hand, lives this way: BE — DO — HAVE.

Winners understand being always precedes doing. In order to succeed, they start by asking: Who do I need to be? What kind of person would have access to those kinds of outcomes? What would I be doing by being that kind of person? Then, they naturally end up having what that person would have. The having takes care of itself.

The way of the Winner is far more counter-cultural and counter-intuitive, yet it's the only way that actually works.

Which way are you currently going about life?

35
Self-talk Programming

Talking to yourself is a very natural part of life. Everyone does it, but most people are quite careless about the kind of conversations that happen internally.

In his book, *What to say when you talk to your self,* Shad Helmstetter says the relationship between our conscious and subconscious is like the captain of the ship and the engine room worker. The captain gives the order and the worker does what they are told.

We give orders to our subconscious by our self-talk. The problem is it's usually very negative. People say things like: *I'm not creative, I'm no good with money, I struggle to make friends.* What happens next is the subconscious goes and works out how to not be creative, not have money and suck at being a friend because that's the instruction it's been given.

The key is to know what you want, and who you would need to be to achieve it. Then you can start talking to yourself like you're that person already.

This kind of self-talk is not just an exercise in positivity, but programming. It's your conscious giving your subconscious a simple instruction about the desired direction you want to head in the future. As a result, successful people are very careful about what they say when talking to themselves.

36
Morning Rituals

Author of *The Miracle Morning,* Hal Elrod, suggests that there are six crucial aspects to the way successful people start their day that differentiate them from the average person. Amazingly, all these practices can be done in as little as six minutes. He has created the SAVERS acronym as a helpful way of remembering all six rituals.

1. Silence: immediately start the day with mindfulness, meditation, centredness, prayer or just simple breathing exercises.

2. Affirmation: ask yourself who do you need to be to succeed and start talking to yourself like you're that person already.

3. Visualisation: see yourself experiencing the results you want now, so that when you get them it won't be a surprise.

4. Exercise: do some short sharp physical activity, such as star jumps or push-ups, to increase oxygen and blood flow to your entire body, especially your brain.

5. Reading: learn something new that will add value to your life

6. Scribing: journaling is a great way of opening the lines of communication with yourself and creating a safe space to listen to what is going on internally.

7. If you want to succeed in life, just notice the power of starting each day well and how it affects your overall results.

37
Pick Yourself

American entrepreneurial legend and bestselling author, Seth Godin[7], says that, too often, people are waiting for someone else to pick them for the team.

While this may have been a good strategy 20 or 30 years ago, it's a recipe for disaster in today's marketplace. In the past, your best bet for getting a good job was to stand out from the crowd with a great education from one of the best universities and then wait for a big company to notice you.

It's not that education is no longer important, but the world has radically changed. With the coming of the internet, YouTube and social media, there's no longer any barrier to entry for someone looking to be seen or heard.

Godin suggests that the most important thing, especially for young people trying to make life work in today's world, is to stop trying to get someone else to pick you and to instead go ahead and pick yourself. In the history of the world, there's never been an easier time to stand up, back yourself, create something beautiful and share it with the world.

Stop waiting to be picked by someone else. It's time to pick yourself!

38
Resourceful Certainty

One of the six core needs is certainty. Craving certainty is all about our desire for comfort, control and safety. We feel certain when things are known and predictable, and nothing is uncertain.

Often, this need is met in really unresourceful ways — bullying, controlling others, being risk-averse, anxiety, self-medication or even self-sabotage. Yet, because this need will not go unmet in our life, the key is to find high-quality, healthy or resourceful ways of meeting the need in a way that's good for us, and others.

The paradox is that we crave certainty in a world full of uncertainty. Therefore, the most resourceful way of meeting the need is to embrace uncertainty and back yourself. It's like saying, I have no idea of what tomorrow will bring, but I have all that I need within me and so I'll work it out when I get there.'

If you expect things to always go perfectly, the moment they don't you become stressed and anxious. Yet if you expect things to be uncertain and ever-changing, when stuff goes wrong or things pop up from nowhere, you're prepared because you expected it.

Instead of trying to find certainty by getting it from others or substances, find it by taking responsibility for the only thing you can control — yourself.

39
Celebrate – Acknowledge – Reward

I've mentioned before that pleasure and pain are two great motivators. Everything we do each moment is either driven by our desire to avoid pain or pursue pleasure.

One of the most important aspects of maintaining a new desired behaviour is something that doesn't seem to come naturally to most people.

Have you ever been to Sea World and watched the dolphins jump through hoops? Imagine how motivated they would be to repeat that trick for the next eager crowd if they failed to receive a fish for their efforts. They'd be like, 'Blow that. You jump through the damn hoop.'

It's not uncommon for people to push themselves really hard, anticipating how great it will feel to complete the task. Yet when they finally do, the overwhelming emotion is more about relief, rather than celebration. 'Ok. Great. That's over. Now what's next?'

The key to getting the best out of yourself is to acknowledge, celebrate and reward the kind of behaviour you are trying to reproduce and maintain. This totally builds the pleasure association with the new behaviour and increases our motivation to do it again.

40
Values and Rules

One of the most essential elements of a happy life is living in line with your values. If something is important to you, yet you find yourself behaving in a way that's different from what you value, it causes deep unhappiness.

Interestingly, every value we have has an associated rule or measurement to let us know when we get a tick in that box. For example, it may be really important for you to be a healthy person, but the question is: What is the rule for health? Do you have to exercise 10 times a week and eat no sugar before you get a tick?

Often people have great values, but really tough, arbitrary rules that are very difficult to achieve. This leaves them feeling unhappy and like they're not living out their values. Therefore, it's important to update the rules to ensure they're not ruining the game.

To review the quality of your rules, it's useful to explore where they came from in the first place and who helped write them for you. Often, people discover they're still following the rules of previous generations, even though they're trying to live their own lives today.

The key is to be clear about the values that are most important to you and then set fantastic rules or measurements that allow you to live in line with these values.

41
No Behaviour Management

When it comes to change and self-improvement, most people only have one strategy: To try harder, be better, just stop it, or to use more effort, energy and focus to behave differently.

Yet this approach can never lead to lasting change. Behaviour is at the end of the assembly line in the factory of our lives. Trying to change your behaviour without dealing with the cause of the behaviour is like trying to kill an apple tree by picking the apples off it. It doesn't even harm the tree, and there will be a whole heap of apples again next season.

Sometimes people think that coaching is all about changing your attitude and just being more positive, but while these band-aid solutions may bring a sense of short-term happiness, they can never bring about long-term change.

It never ceases to amaze me how much hope people seem to place in change strategies that are purely based on behaviour management. 'I'm just going to try harder ... I'm really going to focus on responding differently ... I know I can do better at this ... I'm going to be more assertive and not let this person affect me.'

Genuine transformation comes when we make deep change to the factory that is producing the problem behaviour in the first place. All behaviour, emotion and thinking flows out of our belief system, so true change work always takes place on the level of our core beliefs. When these beliefs are changed, the behaviour automatically takes care of itself.

42
Reframe Safety

I often hear people say that those who succeed in life do so because they have more courage and less fear than the average Jo. I'm convinced that's actually not true. Successful people still have fear — they are just afraid of different things. Instead of fearing failure, rejection and disappointment, they fear anything that's going to undermine their sense of self, keep them small and needy, or leave them with regrets and disappointment.

The key to success is always about reframing what we need to be afraid of. It's just like an overprotective parent. For the sake of love, they instil fear in their child about the big bad world, and then wrap them in cotton wool so they don't get hurt.

Yet as the kids grow older, they begin to realise that the world probably isn't that big and bad. The biggest threat to their safety is their mum, who is actually ruining any chance of them being a healthy adult.

We always need to be safe, but the key question is: What do you really need protection from? When you fear the stuff that keep you from succeeding, then that fear will actually serve to propel you forward into life.

43
The Danger of Confidence

One of the most common outcomes people are looking for in coaching is weight loss. Often people imagine that losing weight will give them more confidence. Yet if that was as simple and good as it sounds, they would have found a way to get this outcome already.

The hidden issue is that there is always some part of them sabotaging or resisting the change process because of how dangerous confidence really is.

This is often quite a surprise to discover. However, until the danger is diminished, they will hang on to the extra weight to avoid getting this confidence. It turns out that a confident person will face a range of hazards and difficulties that an unconfident person will never have to face.

Confident people back themselves, say yes to challenges and put themselves in the spotlight. As a direct result, they get more judgement from others, they fail more, and experience more stress, pressure and uncertainty.

People often imagine that their biggest fear is failure, but failure is common and easy. What's more, we all know how to fail. However, the fear of success is far greater for most people because of how much uncertainty it opens up.

Therefore, in order for it to be safe enough to lose weight and gain confidence, there is some important personal development work to be done first.

44
The Power of Focus

....

Coaching is all about helping people see that we each have 100% choice. While we might not choose the things that happen to us, we always get to choose how we respond. One of the coolest things we get to choose is focus.

The reality is that we can't focus on everything and so, by default, we're always choosing what we focus on. This is an amazing and empowering discovery that helps us to take full responsibility for our results and our emotional state. What we focus on determines what we miss and, also, what we get more of.

Take a moment to notice exactly what you're paying attention to in your life, work, marriage, family and health right now. What you focus on also determines what's hidden. What are you missing? What else could you be focused on?

It's far more common to focus on the things that aren't going well than the things that are good. But why focus on the two mistakes you made last week rather than the ten things you did really well? So what if you can see three people that don't like you? What about the ten who think you're awesome?

This isn't about only focusing on the positives, instead it's an opportunity to notice exactly what you're currently filling your mind with and to examine the impact it's having on every area of your life.

45
People Work Perfectly

When it comes to change, the most common approach is to just stop it, try harder, be better, more disciplined, more focused and more energised. Yet behaviour is at the end of the assembly line. It isn't created in a vacuum. Instead it's produced by a whole bunch of internal frameworks and systems.

If you went to a factory that was producing boxes and noticed the first box on the conveyor belt was missing a side, you'd imagine it was broken. But if every box came out missing the same side, you'd have to believe it was created like that. If you want a box with all the sides on it, you only have two options — change the factory machine or fix the box.

Sadly, the second option is how most people go about change work. They just put sides on boxes. The problem is that there is no end to this cycle. Every box comes out missing the same side, so you have to manually fix every box. Some people seem to have more energy and more capacity for putting sides on boxes than others, but ultimately it's a fool's quest.

There is no point using behaviour management as your change strategy. Just with the box, it's futile to judge the box for missing a side and futile to try and change the box. If you want a different result, change the factory that is producing the result in the first place and the end result will automatically change. The same is true in our lives. Change the beliefs and the behaviour takes care of itself.

46
The Gift of Doubt

One of the ways we continue to justify living in a disempowering story is by the abundance of evidence we gather to prove that our story is indeed true. Yet, our evidence doesn't really prove anything because we'll find it for whatever we believe to be true. That's how our brain works.

A belief merely tells our brain which evidence is important to us and serves no purpose to our lives. This means that the vast amount of information available to us in any one moment is ignored.

Therefore, doubt serves as a wonderful gift because it opens our minds to a world of new and different possibilities.

The question is: What else is true? What other evidence also exists that we have been deleting and distorting? The gift of doubt is so useful because it allows us to step back from our concrete world of evidence and see what we've been missing the whole time.

So now the issue is not whether our beliefs are true — because how could we know? It's whether our beliefs are helpful and getting us more of what we want.

47
Hurtfulness

The only people who have the ability to hurt us are those we need something from.

The moment you need something from someone else, they then have the ability to withhold it from you. This gives them the power to make you happy when you get what you need or upset when you don't.

When you put someone in charge of meeting the deep needs in your life, you also risk becoming afraid of them whenever you cannot control them. You have to play their game and keep them happy in order to get what you need from them.

So often people need affirmation, acceptance, love, recognition, significance and security from others, and they have no Plan B to get it elsewhere. Even though they suffer and complain about being treated poorly by these people, until they deal with the external neediness, they will remain trapped in these relationship power plays.

The bad behaviour is so hurtful simply because you have to keep tolerating it! Obviously then, the key to being free is to find internal ways of meeting our needs rather than depending on others.

48
Perception

Did you know that the problem is not actually the problem, but what you think about the problem? Often people act as victims of their circumstances and feel dictated to by the problems happening around them. Yet it is always our perception of the problem that's the issue rather than the situation itself.

The problem is *not* that you have no money — it's that now you feel like a failure and want to give up.

The problem is *not* that this person doesn't like you — it's that you believe their harsh criticism and now feel depressed.

The problem is *not* that your loved one has died — it's that you feel any sense of enjoyment in life would now seem somehow inappropriate and so your life has practically ended too.

Holocaust survivor, Viktor Frankl, powerfully demonstrated this reality. He discovered that between what happens to us and how our life is affected, there is always a choice. We get to choose how we'll respond.

Rather than feeling controlled by your current problems, take a breath and realise that the problem is not the problem, but what you think about that problem. And this, you can change.

49
Being Too Hasty

I love the story from the movie, *Charlie Wilson's War*.[8]

A young boy gets a horse for his birthday and everybody in the village says, 'How wonderful. The boy finally got the horse he has always wanted.' The Zen master says, 'We'll see.'

Soon after, the boy falls off the horse and breaks his leg. Everyone in the village says, 'How terrible. He should not have got a horse.' The Zen master says, 'We'll see.'

Then, a war breaks out and all the young men have to go off and fight, except the boy. He can't go because his leg has not healed. The villagers say, 'How wonderful.' The Zen master says, 'We'll see.'

And so it goes on.

The point is it's always difficult to assess the impact something will have on your life in any one moment. Therefore, it's prudent to hold off labelling your experiences as good or bad while you're in the process of having them.

One day, you may look back at the worst day of your life with immense gratitude for how that experience radically altered the path you were walking.

Every moment presents us with life-altering opportunities. If you're too quick to judge the merit of the experience as good or bad, you may miss the gift altogether.

50
Busyness as an Addiction

Busyness is one of the most socially acceptable but harmful addictions of our world today. It has the capacity to meet all six of our core needs — certainty, variety, significance, love, contribution and growth — which is what makes it so addictive! Yet, while filling our life with action and work meets our needs, it does so in a very unhealthy and unsustainable way.

Even though most people try hard not to be so busy, like all addictions, there are a number of factors making it hard to break free.

Busyness is celebrated and rewarded culturally and even built into the way we greet each other — 'How's it going? Busy?' The correct answer is: 'Yeah, so busy I can hardly scratch myself.' If you say no, people wonder what in the world you are doing with your life! Yet, while busyness may benefit you socially, it eventually causes major problems in all other areas of life.

It's so common for people to feel they're defined by what they're able to do. The more they do, the more important and significant they feel. The problem is that when you have nothing to do, or no one is watching what you do, it creates an identity crisis.

The solution is to meet all of your core needs with more high-quality and internal strategies, instead of using busyness as the only means of filling your cup.

51
Course Correction

Did you know that a rocket ship on a long trip to outer space is only on track around 3% of the time? The rest of the time, it's making constant course corrections. It assesses where it is in relation to where it's heading, and then makes the necessary adjustments to get back on track as quickly as possible.

So many people imagine that success is being on track 100% of the time, so the moment they miss a goal, they feel like they've failed and then give up. Yet, if one of the most high-tech machines on the planet is only on track a fraction of the time, maybe there's an important lesson to learn about true success.

The key is to be clear about where you really want to head in life and who you are on your best day. Then calibrate your current position in relation to that ideal. If things are not how you want them to be, then, without judging yourself, simply check in to see what adjustments you need to make to get back on track to be at your best.

People who succeed in life have a high level of behavioural flexibility and are making constant course corrections. They are aware that they will constantly be knocked off course throughout the day but know how to get back on track without feeling like they've failed.

52
Have To vs Choose To

When we operate with the illusion of no choice, we get stuck in situations of obligation where we feel like we have to, need to, or should do a bunch of things we don't want to do.

I *have* to go to work. I *have* to visit my parents. I *have* to provide for my family. I *have* to finish my university degree. I *have* to exercise. I *have* to do what my boss wants.

The reality is that we don't have to do anything. Not that I'm suggesting this is a good idea, but some people don't do any of these things and they get away with it.

Everything is a choice and every choice has consequences. Living with the illusion of no choice and being stuck in obligation can lead to feeling unhappy and even create a sense of hopelessness. When we live out of obligation, everything is done grudgingly with a sense of growing resentment.

Empowered living starts with embracing 100% choice and owning 100% responsibility for the consequences of these choices. This gives us a sense of control over our own lives and enables us to be fully engaged in what we do, rather than just showing up to life because we *have* to.

53
Frustration with Others = Frustration with Self

I had a conversation with my wife recently where I noticed myself getting quite frustrated. She was talking about some stuff she'd been struggling with for quite some time. I started to become quite impatient, thinking to myself, oh man, can't you just sort that out already?

As soon as those thoughts formed in my mind, I realised that my frustration with her was really a cover-up for frustration with myself. It's far easier to get upset at other people's shortcomings, weaknesses or failings than it is to come to terms with your own stuff.

It turns out that I had some stuff in my life that I still hadn't worked out how to overcome either, and I was disappointed and frustrated about it. My wife's sharing just reminded me of my own struggles.

The things that get on our nerves and annoy us most in others actually exist inside us, otherwise we wouldn't notice them. The old saying, 'It takes one to know one', rings true in this case.

So the next time you find yourself getting frustrated with others, take a moment to check what you're really upset about in your own life first. Deal with the BBQ sauce stain on your own shirt before you point fingers at other people's shirt stains. Frustration with others is always an indication of frustration with self.

54
The Problem with Positivity

It's common for people to believe that positivity is the solution to every problem.

Often people imagine that life coaching is all about a kick up the bum to change your attitude and become more positive about your situation. This is actually far from the truth.

Interestingly, not everything in life is positive. If you pretend that negative things are really positive things, then life becomes about lying and hiding from reality. This means that, at the end of the day, the balance sheet of life just doesn't add up and you have to cover the costs personally! Sometimes the most important and healthy thing you can do is stop and say, 'Actually, this isn't right. This isn't ok. I'm not happy about this. Stop behaving like this. I won't tolerate this anymore.'

It seems really cool and noble to be an ultra-positive person, but often these kinds of people are covering up a whole bunch of negatives with a fake smile. It's just not sustainable.

It's OK to have a bad day sometimes, to feel flat and unsettled or uneasy. Coming to terms with negatives and being honest, rather than trying to sugar coat life, always leads to more personal growth and deeper maturity as a human being.

55
Your Body Knows

One of the things I enjoy most about the coaching space is the concept of developing rapport with self. That might sound strange, but it's no different or less important than developing deep relationships with others.

So much about flourishing in life comes out of learning to love, respect, listen to and understand ourselves, rather than trying to fight against ourselves to get the best results.

You get the best out of others when you love and trust them. The same is true when getting the best out of yourself. So often, I watch people try to flog themselves to death through effort, discipline and more focus. This may work in the short term but can ultimately leave you at war with yourself.

I was coaching a woman recently who had battled chronic illness for seven years. Every six months, she seemed to pick up some new, rare disease or sickness.

Through the coaching process, she discovered that this sickness was actually an attempt to get her to stop and rest. She had embarked on a crazy journey, hell bent on proving herself to her mother, and hadn't made any space for rest. The only time she stopped was when she was sick.

Learning to listen to herself and hear what her body was saying meant she could find a much more sustainable way to factor rest into her life and let go of the sickness altogether.

56
Mindfulness – Be External

One of the central differences between animals and humans is the ability we have for self-awareness. Animals act from impulse and instinct, whereas we are able to think about our thinking and observe our own behaviour.

Yet so often people operate with such limited self-awareness. They go on doing what they've always done without ever stopping to review, understand and evaluate the path they're on.

Mindfulness may sound like a weird new-age term, but it's simply the exercise of observing our own thoughts and emotions. It is to position yourself outside your own life, looking in. Therefore, mindfulness is an essential part of fully 'being' human.

It's an incredibly useful practice, as the act of separating yourself from your own thinking and feeling means you're then able to choose what to do with those very thoughts and emotions, rather than living as a slave to whatever comes into your mind.

Take a moment to stop and observe your own life today and you'll be amazed at how powerful and useful self-awareness really is.

57
Be the Prize

....

In his bestselling book, *Influence*, Robert Cialdini describes the powerful impact the law of scarcity has on human behaviour. We want what we can't have. The more we can't have it, or the harder it is to obtain, the more we want it. Whereas we seem to be a bit blasé about those things in life that are freely available, cheap or easy, and rarely appreciate their value. Awareness of this is crucial when it comes to interpersonal relationships.

Before two people start dating, for example, the perceived value of each person is massive. The aim is to woo and pursue them with the goal of winning their heart, even though there's no guarantee you'll succeed. Once a relationship is established and you spend lots of time together, however, it's easy to become familiar with each other.

Yet the moment you stop becoming the prize, your perceived value diminishes. It becomes common to be taken for granted, overlooked or, in the worst case, used and abused. People who no longer feel like the prize become needy and desperate, which is actually very unattractive in life, business and relationships.

Successful relationships of any kind depend on you being the prize. This requires you to fully own your true value and worth, rather than showing up needy and desperate.

58
Everything can be Reframed

Every experience in our lives can be reframed because everything is framed in the first place.

We think we see the world as it is, yet five people observing the same event will all perceive and experience it differently. The problems in our lives are not the problem. The problem is what we think about the problem. Today's problem, in the light of today, is massive. The same problem, in light of this year, isn't as big. The problem, in light of your entire lifetime, disappears completely.

We see the world through a lens or a frame. It filters our experience of life and colours our understanding of what's actually taking place. When we change the frame we're looking through, we also completely change our experience.

Here are some cool frame examples to try. What am I grateful for right now? What would my hero do in this situation? What would my 10-year-old self tell me right now? What if I had no fear? What if I only had six months to live? In ten years time, what will I remember about this problem?

Everything can be reframed. Choose the frame that gets you more of what you want in each situation.

59
Quality Questions

Anthony Robbins says that the quality of our life is determined by the quality of the questions we ask ourselves.[9] Low-quality questions lead to a low-quality experience of life.

Nick Vujicic,[10] a man born without arms and legs, turned his life around by changing the quality of his internal questions. Instead of asking the typical 'Why me?' he asked, 'How can I use the way that I look to get more of what I want?' This enabled him to reframe his birth disability to become his unfair advantage.

He desired to be a motivational speaker and could see that he was competing with many others for a few opportunities, yet this high-quality question allowed him to see that he could jump the queue because of his appearance! He used this same strategy to marry his gorgeous wife.

Here are some other great high-quality questions:

Instead of asking *how* am I going to make this work, ask *why* must I find a way to make this work and *why* is this so important?

Instead of *how* can I get more money, ask *how* can I add the most value to as many people as possible today?

Instead of asking *what* do I need to do to get ahead, ask *who* do I need to be to achieve my dreams and what would I be doing if I was being that kind of person?

What high-quality questions can you ask yourself today?

60
Smarter Goals

Being happy and successful starts with a very clear description of exactly what you mean by happiness and success. There must be a clear and tangible picture of the goal you have in mind, otherwise it's impossible to achieve.

Simply stating that you want to be happy and successful is never enough. In fact, using vague and abstract language sets you up for failure and disappointment instead. Effective goal setting requires a number of crucial elements best characterised by the *Smarter* framework[11].

1. Specific: start by being as specific as possible about what you want.

2. Measurable: set clear measurements that indicate whether you have achieved the goal or not.

3. Attractive: make sure it's important and desirable to you.

4. Realistic: although all goals should stretch us, it must still be realistic.

5. Time bound: set parameters for when it will be completed.

6. Ecological: make sure the goal is good for you and good for the world.

7. Resources: make sure you have the resources available to achieve this goal.

Using the *Smarter* framework is a great way to create well-formed outcomes. Remember, the harder you work when setting the goal, the easier achieving the goal becomes.

61
Problem – Remedy – Outcome

One of the most important aspects of living life well is to be focused on the outcomes that are most important to you.

However, it is often the case that people are either problem focused, or remedy focused instead. Neither of these focus points have the ability to lead to life. When a person comes to me focused on a problem — for example, their work is unfulfilling — my aim is to move them to an outcome focus by simply asking, 'What would you like to have happen instead?'

When someone comes with a remedy — for example, they've decided they need to move to Bali — I again move them to an outcome by asking, 'Then what will happen? What do you imagine moving to Bali will give you?'

This is a great exercise to use with yourself. These are simple questions that will move you out of being focused on what's wrong with the situation or being focused on random solutions or remedies. The aim is always to be clear about what you're trying to achieve first. Moving to an outcome focus makes sure you create remedies that genuinely solve the problems you're facing.

62
Perceptual Positions

A great conflict resolution strategy is the use of a variety of perceptual positions[12] — first person, second person, third person.

During conflict, it's natural to only see the situation though your own eyes (first person). But imagine stepping out of your body and having a look at the conflict through the eyes of the other party (second person). Imagine how they would be feeling and what they would be seeing. Observing the conflict through their eyes would look very different than looking through yours. This change in perspective allows you to gain insights you were previously oblivious to about the situation.

Now imagine stepping into the shoes of an innocent bystander who was simply observing the conflict and had no vested interest in the outcome (third person). What would you feel or see looking at the conflict through their eyes?

The process of changing your perception of the conflict, by moving between first person, second person and third person, always gives you more information. Having more information always opens new pathways for the conflict to be resolved.

Changing vantage points takes courage and humility, and you may be surprised at what you discover.

63
Taking the Handbrake Off

When it comes to making lasting personal change and self-improvement, it's common for people to have a really unhelpful metaphor in mind to represent this journey.

Typically, people imagine success in this area is like climbing to the top of a snow-capped mountain to capture the flag. Looking up from the foot of this mountain, they can barely even see the peak through the clouds. To get to the top means trekking through dense forest, followed by rocks, ice and snow.

To make matters worse, it's super windy and steep and they wonder if they have what it takes to make it, even on their best day. If they were to get halfway up, there's no guarantee they'd make it any higher. The moment they stop climbing, they could fall back down the mountain. It's such a demoralising picture that it causes many to continue putting off the trek altogether.

The great news is that growth, success and happiness are actually nothing like that. A far more accurate metaphor to describe the personal change journey, is to see yourself sitting on top of a hill in a parked car with the handbrake on. The flag is at the bottom of the hill. All that's between you and the goal is that brake. You actually have everything you need already — you're just holding yourself back through internal doubts, fears and limiting beliefs.

Growth and success is actually all about dealing with the handbrake, rather than fighting your way up a mountain.

64
Highest Common Agreement

Conflict in relationships is often played out on the lowest level of disagreement. When people argue about things they'll never agree about, it can seem like there's no way forward. In order to resolve the conflict, however, the conversation needs to move to the highest common agreement instead. In every conflict situation, there's always something both sides agree on. Finding this agreement opens up the ability to negotiate about the disagreement.

I once worked with a trucking company where two of the mechanics were at war over the radio. One always wanted to turn it up, the other always wanted to turn it off. They were never going to agree with each other. When I asked the first mechanic why it was important to have it loud, he told me it helped him be in a good mood at work, which made him enjoy his role and be an effective part of the team.

The second mechanic explained that the purpose behind having no music was to allow him to better concentrate on his job. This was important to him because he wanted to do a good job and play his part in the team to the best of his ability.

Amazingly, both men wanted exactly the same thing. Once they saw this, it then opened up the ability to negotiate and find a win-win situation that they'd never seen before.

Finding the highest common agreement is always the key to resolving conflict.

65
Dispassionate Observer

One of the most crucial aspects of all personal growth is self-awareness. You can't change what you can't see! Yet, people typically operate with a very limited level of self-awareness and rarely explore what's really going on in their lives.

When a person begins to reflect on their behaviour in an attempt to increase self-awareness, often they do it as the critic or the drill sergeant. They imagine that shaming themselves, disapproving or trying to force themselves to toughen up and just get it sorted will bring about change.

The internal critic, or the drill sergeant, never brings about lasting change because they come from a place of judgement. This causes us to shut down and hide, which further suppresses what' is happening beneath the surface. It proves to be impossible to do self-judgement and self-awareness at the same time.

One of the best ways to reflect on your own life, therefore, is to be a dispassionate observer. This means you have no agenda, no judgement and no opinion — only curiosity. The moment you show up like this, all of a sudden it becomes totally safe to explore any area of your life.

66
Ego and Awareness Cannot Coexist

Eckhart Tolle says that the ego is the unobserved mind.[13] That is, when we run on autopilot, doing whatever we think or feel in the moment, the ego thrives and totally takes over. Our ego is the part of us that always needs to compare ourselves with others or prove our value and worth to the world. As such, the ego definitely causes us to behave out our worst.

This is why self-awareness is so important. The simple act of stopping and observing your own thoughts or emotions stops our ego in its tracks. Rather than allowing thoughts and emotions to go unchecked, practising self-awareness enables us to realise that we are not just the product of our thoughts and emotions. We have the ability to choose what we do with them.

Ego and awareness can't operate in the same place at the same time. Stopping, breathing, observing ourselves and becoming aware of what we are thinking and feeling means we're then able to exercise choice and responsibility for our lives. This gets us out of our ego and allows us to operate as our true self.

If reflection, silence, journaling, meditation and asking yourself great questions are not part of your daily rhythm, today may be a great time to start.

67
Wanting

Have you ever noticed that conversations with friends and family about change rarely bring about change?

We all want our friends and family to be happy and make great choices, yet it turns out that wanting someone to change, grow or make healthy choices may in fact be the least effective way of positively influencing them.

Think about the conversations you've had with your parents, your kids or your friends, particularly when one of you have made a suggestion about what should or shouldn't be happening. While intentions may be good, the problem is that it's actually all about what you want and therefore a form of judgement.

We want, or even need, others to do and be certain things to make ourselves feel better about our own lives. The major problem is that when we communicate this wanting to those we love, deep down its always perceived as a judgement. It's imposing your views, expectations, rules and map of reality onto another.

Wanting someone to do something, even for all the right reasons, only produces expectation, obligation, pressure and judgement. This is only ever an external and temporary form of motivation. Lasting motivation is always internally driven.

68
Negotiability

Often people imagine they're far more negotiable than they really are. It's common for people to feel like they have real options on the table in front of them when really, they're only ever going to choose what they've always chosen.

Instead of actually weighing up the options and finding the best way forward for them, they get stuck living out of obligation and meeting other people's expectations of what they should or shouldn't do. They will, therefore, continue along the exact same road.

The person who is actually free to pick the best path for themselves *and* is highly negotiable has the following qualities:

1. They don't need the approval of others to feel like a good person.

2. They're not defined by their past.

3. They take full responsibility for their own results.

4. They're not defined by what they do, what they have or what they get from others.

5. They have internal reference points for significance, worth and love, and don't seek to have those needs met externally.

6. They're able to say yes because they're fully prepared to say no.

7. How negotiable are you really?

69
Fear is Irrational

Fear is an amazing thing. It's a core part of being alive. The moment we no longer experience some measure of fear is the moment we're no longer drawing breath.

People who succeed in life don't do so because they have less fear and more courage than the average person, they just fear different things.

One of the coolest things about fear is that it's highly irrational. For the most part, we fear weird stuff that doesn't make sense. Kids don't fear the monster under their bed, they fear the *thought* of a monster under their bed. Those with a phobia of flying hold onto this fear even though, in terms of transport, you're far more likely to die driving, riding your bike or being a pedestrian.

One of the things I love most about coaching is that it's all about turning lights on and helping people see what was previously in the dark. If you can't see what you're really afraid of, the fear takes on a life of its own and becomes a massive issue. Fear unobserved always grows. Irrational fear is always diminished the more it's observed.

If fear is natural and necessary, then the key is not to eradicate all fear, but to make sure we're afraid of the right things.

70
Emotional Stability

I've got friends whose main goal in life is emotional consistency. Somewhere along the line they've equated being emotional with weakness and so pride themselves on always being stable and rational. In the process, they've shut down their emotions so there are no peaks or troughs to their daily experience.

While the idea of 'flat-lining' through life greatly appeals to these friends, it has never been something I've aspired to. Sure, they may avoid dark times and periods of emotional instability with this shut down strategy, but if you rule out the lows, you also rule out the highs.

We are emotional beings and all emotions serve an important purpose. People who flourish in life give themselves permission to experience the full spectrum of emotions available to humans. They're not afraid of bad days, pain, sadness, anger, frustration or disappointment because it makes the joy, beauty and excitement of good days all the sweeter. They know that to stand on top of mountains also means walking through deep valleys.

If you're the kind of person who flat-lines through life, maybe it's time to do what The Tin Man did in *The Wizard of Oz*[14] and go on a journey to find the ability to feel again.

71
Framing Expectations

In order to maintain great relationships, it's really important to always frame other people's expectations of you.

Too often, people overpromise and underdeliver in an attempt to keep others happy, inevitably leading to disappointment and broken expectations. We suffer greatly when our expectations go unmet, so this always creates bad feelings towards the person who let you down.

After ordering a meal at a restaurant recently, I was told that there would be a small delay on my food. I quizzed the waiter about what he meant by 'small' and reluctantly he told me I would be waiting 30 minutes. As soon as my expectations had been framed, I was totally ok to wait. If I hadn't gained this clarity, then I may have been imagining 'small' to mean 10 minutes and would have spent 20 minutes being totally frustrated about the long delay. As it turned out, the meal arrived after only 25 minutes and I was really pleased!

Instead of trying to impress people with promises we have no ability to deliver, or being vague to avoid initial disappointment, the key is to clearly communicate the exact reality of your situation and your capabilities to deliver. Then, simply do what you said. This creates great experiences for you and those you interact with.

72
The Importance of Having Bad Days

Did you realise that one of the key ingredients to living a successful life is having more bad days?

There are many people who give themselves zero permission to have bad days. In their minds, positivity is king, performance is everything and consistency is the ultimate goal. However, this is only because their identity has become enmeshed with always looking good, so to have a bad day is an indictment on them personally. A bad day must mean they're a bad person, and so must be avoided at all costs.

Yet, it turns out that bad days are a vital part of a healthy lifestyle and that success is not at all about being on track 100% of the time. In fact, if everything is always good, then you have no idea of what 'good' really is. The universe exists in polarity for a reason. Without night there's no day, without positive and negative charged ions there is no flow of electricity and without cold how would you know what's hot?

If you never allow yourself to experience lows, then it's also impossible to rise to new heights. Here are three keys to integrate more bad days into your life while avoiding the traps.

1. Cut the cord between what you do and who you are. This frees you to have a real experience of life rather than the one you're supposed to have.

2. Manage your energy not your time. Success is about being at your best only when it matters most.

3. Let bad days be a gift. Pain, frustration and discomfort give you clarity about what you don't want and provide vital lessons for self-improvement.

73
The Shadow Effect

One of the great internal battles we face is the fight between our perception of good and evil. In order to win this war, it often seems that people are on a spiritual quest to have God take away their ability to do the wrong thing.

The problem with this is the moment you lose the ability to do the wrong thing, you also lose the ability to choose the right thing. If you had to do the right thing, how can you say you were good? It's only good because you had every chance to do the wrong thing yet made a great choice instead.

Deepak Chopra says that we need our shadow[15] — it's what makes us human. The aim of the game, therefore, is to become aware of what's going on inside us, and our capacity for good and evil, and then to keep making better choices. There's no point judging our shadow or trying to kill it.

What makes choice so wonderful is how real and high the stakes are. We're entirely capable of using our will to *hurt* others and ourselves, or to *help* others and ourselves.

It's an incredible and extraordinary thing to wake up each morning as a human being with a fresh set of choices laid out before us. Those who flourish in life never lose the ability to make a mess of things. That's what makes a life well lived all the more impressive.

74
The Body Craves Health

When it comes to improving the quality of your health, it's typical to imagine you need to fight against your body to win. However, this proves to be a very ineffective and unkind strategy that ends up ruining the relationship you have with yourself.

Weight loss is a classic example. It's as though people imagine they have a fat lazy person inside them who loves Mars Bars and hates exercise, and the aim of the game is to kill that part through as much punishment and cruelty as possible.

I understand the intention to try and motivate yourself to be at your best, but the strategy is brutal and horrible. Imagine if you treated another person the way you treat yourself! Thankfully, there are laws against that.

The key to health is to realise it's our default position. It's home. Our body craves health, and when we learn to listen, trust and respect ourselves, the natural implication is we move towards health.

75
Anyone can be Beautiful

One of my good friends has always told herself, and others, that she's just not beautiful. This has become the story she lives out of, so she never takes care of her appearance, health or weight and then discovers that people confirm this story by telling her she's fat and ugly.

The amazing thing is that anyone can be beautiful if they want to be. You just have to give yourself permission to make the most of what you've got. It's not about being a particular weight, size, height, age or body shape. It's simply about believing that what's inside you is wonderfully valuable and then showing up as the best version of yourself for all to see.

There's always something compelling and attractive about a person who is relaxed, comfortable in their own skin and has allowed themselves to shine. No matter what they look like, they are genuinely beautiful.

When your inner world is at peace, it radiates outward through your eyes. True beauty is being willing to be seen for who you are rather than hiding your light under a basket. There's only one of you in the world — and that makes you beautiful. All you need to do is believe it and the world will see it too.

76
Emotions

Emotions are a funny thing. Sometimes it can feel like they're in control of us and we're just along for the ride. I frequently hear people explain that they didn't choose to feel like this, their emotions just took over!

Yet, while we may not directly get to choose the emotion we're experiencing, we do get to choose the things that create emotional responses in the first place.

One of the most important breakthroughs I've had in my life was realising I could control my emotions simply by what I focused my attention on. Here's a great exercise to prove to yourself just how much control of your emotions you really do have.

Go for a walk and give yourself 10 minutes to experience 10 different emotional states. For example, what would you need to focus on to be instantly angry, frustrated, excited, peaceful, grateful, joyful or sad?

By becoming aware that what you're focusing your attention on directly affects your emotional state, you have the direct capacity to control and change the emotion you're experiencing. When an emotional response isn't serving you well, change your focus and the emotion will follow suit.

77
Success

I'm convinced that succeeding in life is actually quite easy, simply because most people never will. The reality is, you only have to do a few key things well, semi-consistently, and it quickly separates you from the crowd.

Here are a few key things that will quickly help you differentiate from those around you:

1. Be clear about what you want in life.

2. Develop the ability to manage your state so you can show up at your best when it matters most.

3. Become secure in who you are and learn to back yourself.

4. Let go of blame and excuse for poor results.

5. Embrace 100% responsibility and choice.

6. Go where the life is, rather than always playing it safe.

7. Cultivate deep friendships.

8. Give yourself full permission to flourish.

This list of qualities is not complicated, but neither is it easy. For that reason, most people are not willing to become this kind of person.

I'm not sure if you've noticed, but the road less travelled is in no danger of being trampled and overrun by the masses. Every day, we each have access to everything we need to live well, but most people will choose to ignore it and keep doing what they've always done.

78
Let go of Unhappiness

Feeling unhappy is never fun, but the typical strategies to seek happiness again are often very ineffective.

Normally, the first option is to look outside of ourselves for someone or something to make us happy. To deal with negative emotions, stress and anxiety, we often reach for an external fix. Yet, hoping for the world to make us happy when we're feeling blue is only ever a short-term strategy at best.

External solutions can only ever momentarily suppress our internal pain. In the future, the same feelings, or even more intense ones, re-emerge.

The second ineffective strategy is to postpone happiness until we arrive at a certain place. The hope is that when we're in a better situation, or have achieved a goal, then we'll be happy. If and when we do arrive, however, happiness again proves to be very short lived.

Eckhart Tolle says that you can't find happiness by chasing it.[16] When you get where you think happiness is waiting, it eludes you again. Instead of chasing happiness, the key is to let go of unhappiness. It turns out that we already have all we need to be happy, but it's hidden behind fear, doubt, frustration, anxiety and expectation.

You could be happy here and now if you wanted to. In fact, that's the only place you can truly be happy.

79
Don't Confuse Simple with Easy

The path to success is often simple and hard. People quite often imagine their problems are incredibly complicated and totally unique.

The beautiful reality is that they are neither. The solution may not be easy, but it will definitely not be complicated. Although our issues are uniquely fingerprinted, we all go through the same basic issues in very similar ways.

For example, while a great golf swing is technically very simple, it's certainly not easy to achieve. It's both simple and hard. The key to success is to stick to elegantly simple ideas consistently until they change you from the inside out.

I'm sure that over the course of your life, you have been exposed to enough life-changing ideas to transform you 10 times over. When it appears this wisdom doesn't work, however, the problem isn't with the idea but with your application of the idea.

Often, people get bored or distracted and chase the latest trend or new idea instead. However, people who do life well stick to elegantly simple wisdom and truth until it produces fruit in their lives.

80
Everything is Created Twice

One of my all-time favourite ideas from Stephen Covey is that everything is created twice.[17] Everything is first created in the unseen world, either by design or by default, and then the second creation is simply the physical manifestation of what has already been created.

Therefore, if you don't intentionally create a program capable of getting you the results you desire, you'll be living out of the default programming someone else has installed in your brain.

You don't get a great marriage just because it's something you say you want. A great marriage comes as the result of you intentionally and deliberately creating a program or vision for a great marriage in your mind, heart and beliefs first, and then living out of that.

People often lack the awareness to see the default programs they're living out of — inevitably leading to terrible results. Covey says that success comes when we begin with the end in mind and work our way back. We take full responsibility for the fact we are not merely actors in the drama of our life story, but the director, producer and author as well.

If you don't like the results you're currently getting, realise they're not random or coincidental. Everything is created twice! To change your results in the real world, you need to change them in the unseen world first.

81
Do You Want to be Well?

There is this cool story in the Bible about this magic kind of pool that sick people used to camp around in hope of being healed. The story goes that, once a year, an angel would appear and stir the water. The first person to dip a toe in would be totally healed.

There's this paralysed guy who's camped near the pool for 30 years, waiting to be healed. One day, Jesus walks by and asks him if he'd like to be well. It seems like a strange question. I mean, of course he does — right? He's totally committed to being rid of this condition that has afflicted him for most of his life.

That's the beauty of the question. Essentially, Jesus is saying this: If you want to be well, then pick up your mat and walk out of here. But be careful. If you genuinely want to be well, then you can't be defined as the sick guy who has no responsibility and has everyone else care for him. You'll have to step up and function in the real world, fend for yourself and take full responsibility for your own life. If that's what you want, then you can have it now — magic pool or not.

I'm not saying that sickness isn't real. It's just that sometimes we can be hanging onto it more than it's hanging on to us. It's amazing what we can let go of when we're ready to be free.

82
Getting Back Up Again

Life can be brutally tough sometimes. We all face occasions where hard times get the better of us, and all we feel like doing is giving up or giving in.

Over the years, there have been many amazing things written about what to do when your back is to the wall. Here are a few of my favourites:

1. No matter what's happening, you can effectively fight the battles of today. It's only when you add the relentless pressure of yesterday and tomorrow that you start to become overwhelmed. Be present to today. Live one day at a time.

2. Realise it's not the experience of today that devastates you, but the regret and resentment about something that happened yesterday, or the fear and dread of what tomorrow might bring.

3. When you stop worrying about what you can't control, you have time to change what you can control. And that changes everything.

4. If you never go after your dream again, you'll never have it. If you never ask again, the answer will always be no. If you never step forward again, you're stuck right where you are.

If you're in the midst of a battle right now, then these words are for you.

83
Letting Go of *Should*

One of the most negative and destructive words in the English language is *should*.

Should feels like it's capable of motivating us to do better, but instead it fills us with guilt, shame, obligation and judgement. *Should* doesn't have the power to improve anything. Instead, it lies to us and robs us of life.

I love this from Marc and Angel Chernoff's blog:[18]

If you are sitting there thinking things should be different right now, take a deep breath. That's not true and you know it. If it were true, things would be different right now.

Looking back over your past and thinking you *should* have done that better, or you *could* have done that differently, is such an abstract conversation. You did what you did. If you could have done better, you would have.

It's like the ideal you is judging the real you. You did exactly what your beliefs, thoughts and emotions allowed at the time. It doesn't necessarily justify what you did or make it ok. It just takes all the judgement out of it.

The only usefulness in looking back at past behaviour is to understand the intention of why you did what you did so you can take full responsibility for your life and have more choice about what you're going to do today.

84
Humility

I'm sure that most people would agree that humility is a very noble and attractive quality to have in life.

As Aussies, we love that we are honest, hardworking and down to earth. Our culture places humility as a very important virtue but trying to keep people humble by tearing down tall poppies and high achievers is definitely taking things too far.

True humility is to have an appropriate view of yourself without anything to prove or defend. It is not to beat yourself down and underplay who you are, nor is it to overplay your hand and think more highly of yourself than you ought. If you're actually the best in your chosen field, it's a humble act to fully be that person.

One of the most profound quotes on the subject comes from author, spiritual leader and political activist, Marianne Williamson[19]. She says:

We ask ourselves, who am I to be brilliant, gorgeous, talented, fabulous? Actually, who are you not to be all those things? You are a child of God. Your playing small does not serve the world. There is nothing enlightened about shrinking so that other people won't feel insecure around you. We are all meant to shine, and as we let our own light shine, we unconsciously give other people permission to do the same.

Now that is the essence of humility.

85
The Power of Visualisation

Every day, I talk to people who are hoping to improve their lives. The problem is that hope is not a plan. Just hoping things will somehow miraculously get better is no way to make things actually get better.

One of the most important aspects of improving your results in any area of life is through visualisation. You've actually got to be able to see the results you're looking for in your mind's eye and feel they are real before you'll ever achieve them. If you can't clearly picture yourself having or doing the things you say you want to achieve, then it will only ever remain a hope, prayer or dream.

Top sports people are incredibly disciplined at seeing themselves achieve the kind of results they want, long before the game even arises. Top golfers take a moment to visualise the ball going exactly where they'd like it to before they step up to the tee. This practice is scientifically proven to increase accuracy and performance. Visually rehearsing seeing yourself hitting the ball straight creates the same neural pathways as physically hitting golf balls successfully!

When it comes to your life, the principle is exactly the same. Practise seeing your life the way you want it to be, rather than just hoping things will improve.

86
Social Skills

One of the most important aspects of doing life well is the ability to connect meaningfully with other people.

Whether it comes naturally to you or not, social skills can be learnt and improved. Social confidence largely exists only in people's imaginations. The difference between pretending to be confident and actually being confident is very hard to tell.

You may be tempted to avoid social interactions because you think you lack social skills, but unfortunately, this only ensures you keep lacking social skills. The key to improving them is to interact with others no matter how capable you are right now. Try these tips when interacting with others:

5. Walk, talk, dress, sit and stand as though you are confident — whether you feel like it or not.
6. Ask open questions, then actually listen to the answers.
7. Be interested in other people and what's important to them.
8. Make a point of remembering people's names.
9. Get some skin in the game — shake hands, fist pump, high five, kiss, hug.
10. Listen more than you talk.
11. Ask for feedback from those who care about you.
12. Hang out with people who are socially smooth.
13. Most importantly, keep working on your relationship with yourself. Insecurity and constantly needing the approval of others to feel good about yourself undermines social skills more than anything else.

87
The Power of Imagination

Albert Einstein said that imagination is more important than knowledge.[20] One hems us in by the limits of what is. The other gives freedom to roam among the possibilities of what might be.

The person with the big dreams is more powerful than the one with all the facts. Holocaust survivor, Viktor Frankl, realised that although his Nazi captors had his body, they could not contain his mind. Because of the ability of imagination, he could transport himself anywhere in the world.

Our thoughts have the power to affect every area of our life. For example, imagine you have a lemon in front of you right now. See yourself slicing it in two, bringing one of the halves slowly towards your mouth and then biting into it, skin and all. It's incredible that just the imagination of that motion triggers all the same bodily responses as if we were actually doing the real thing.

The power of imagination to shape our experience of life is extraordinary.

88
Coping with Disappointment

CS Lewis is one of my favourite authors. The movie, *Shadowlands*,[21] shares his painful journey of finally finding love late in life. Only two years after getting married, he lost his wife to cancer.

His deep sorrow after her death led him to reflect on the fact that if he'd never opened his heart and fallen in love in the first place, he wouldn't be experiencing all this pain.

Yet, in spite of the intense grief and loss, he resolves that, given the same choice over, he would again choose love.

Lewis says,

To love at all is to be vulnerable. Love anything and your heart will be wrung and possibly broken. If you want to make sure of keeping it intact, you must give it to no one, not even an animal. Wrap it carefully round with hobbies and little luxuries; avoid all entanglements. Lock it up safe in the casket or coffin of your selfishness. But in that casket, safe, dark, motionless, airless, it will change. It will not be broken; it will become unbreakable, impenetrable, irredeemable. To love is to be vulnerable.[22]

Pain is part of love. As Alfred, Lord Tennyson famously said: 'Tis better to have loved and lost than never loved at all.'[23]

89
Comparison

Comparing yourself with others is such a normal, yet dangerous, thing to do.

For example, it's not uncommon for schools to promote a spirit of excellence in their students to try and motivate them. The only problem is that excellence comes from the word 'to excel'. It's a comparison word. It means to be better than someone or something. Only one or two can be excellent by the very definition of the word. Only one can win the race or top the class, the rest are just not excellent.

When we compare ourselves with others, we feel the need to compete. The problem is that no matter how good we are, there's always someone who can do something better than us.

Comparison is a low-quality attempt from our ego to try and make ourselves feel significant. It's a horrible strategy and it leads to putting others down to get ahead of them.

Instead, you've got to focus on making the most of what you've been given. Be the best you can be. Stop comparing yourself to others and run your own race. You're already significant.

90
Winning is Better than Losing

Experiencing failure, disappointment and loss is a natural and unavoidable part of life.

As such, every business owner, sporting club and aspiring leader understands the value of staying focused, positive and keeping a good attitude when they're losing so they don't give up prematurely.

The truth is, however, it's so much easier to have a great attitude when you're winning! As obvious as it sounds, winning is actually better than losing.

Winning is important and necessary. Don't imagine you can survive without it. Before you pour your heart into doing what you love and dreaming of how cool it will be to make a difference for others without reference to how well it will work out for you, make sure you've picked an avenue that gives you a great chance of clocking up some really cool wins. (Just to clarify — that's real wins in the real world, not pretend wins in the land of 'it will all work itself out one day'.)

If you're not getting enough wins, eventually you'll be incapable of giving anyone else wins either. Businesses, sporting teams and politicians cannot survive without regular wins. The thing to realise is that neither can you.

Winning is way better than losing. Simple, but profoundly important.

91

The Four A's of Personal Transformation

There are four stages of personal transformation.[24]

Stage 1. Acceptance
Transformation starts with specifically accepting that all we have is story. We're sense-making creatures who go into the world and tell stories about our experiences. We don't see reality, just our perception of reality. The meaning we place on defining moments become the basis for the stories we live out of.

Stage 2. Awareness
If all we have is story, it's essential to have awareness of the specific story you're living out of and where it started. Everything is created twice. Your current results are merely the by-product of the script you've been living out of.

Stage 3. Accountability
This stage is about being accountable to the fact that you're not the actor in the story, you're the storyteller. Transformation happens as you hold yourself accountable to 100% choice and responsibility about the story you would like to live out of. You're not a victim and you get to choose your story.

Stage 4. Adaptation
This stage is simply the fruit of doing the first three stages well. It's impossible not to experience different results. Behaviour, emotion and thought are at the end of the assembly line in the factory of beliefs. Once you make different choices in the moment and don't give the old patterns any energy, your stories will naturally change. Your results will adapt to follow your new thoughts.

92
Unresourceful Variety

....

One of the great challenges of being a human being is how to effectively manage all 24 hours we get given each day. People often find themselves disorganised, forgetful, behind, late, busy and rushed. They procrastinate about the important stuff and waste time on the trivial. Time management becomes a source of great pain and frustration for many, and even though they work hard to improve this area, it proves very difficult to change.

It's no mystery that I think Anthony Robbins' six core needs model provides some of the best insights into human behaviour you'll ever come across. It shines some light onto one interesting reason people experience difficulty with time management.

So often, the mess in people's lives is simply a low-quality subconscious way of meeting the need for variety. Being disorganised or chaotic means there's always plenty of different stuff popping up all the time.

In order to change this, the key is to meet the need for variety more resourcefully. You always need variety in your life, so if you intentionally factor in adventure, hobbies, holidays, learning, meeting new people and trying new things, the unresourceful strategies simply drop out of your life and you lose the need to keep being so disorganised.

93
Aligning Head and Heart

I'm sure there have been times in your life where what's happening in your head and heart don't match. Perhaps you desire something in your heart, but then your head questions if you deserve it. Or maybe something makes sense rationally, but your heart isn't in it.

In his fantastic book, *Breaking the Habit of Being Yourself*, Joe Dispenza[25] says that when our head and heart aren't in alignment, it's a recipe for disaster. There's just no way to get ahead or to achieve great results unless everything inside you is pointing in the same direction. If our head and heart want different things, one simply sabotages the other and neither wins.

Navigating head–heart misalignment requires a commitment to work with yourself rather than against yourself. This is why conversations with yourself are so important.

One of my most valuable rituals is a weekly meeting with myself to check in and see what my head *and* heart are saying. Keeping the lines of communication open then allows me to make the necessary adjustments to get them pointing in the same direction.

What are your head and heart saying right now? Are they working together or heading in opposite directions?

94
If You Don't Know What You Want

To have desire is a central part of what makes us human. The Proverb[26] says that when our heartfelt desires are fulfilled it's like a tree of life. Yet, hope deferred makes the heart sick.

I always find it surprising, therefore, when people aren't in touch with what they truly desire for their lives. Yet so many people don't know what they want!

I get that it's safe to settle for what you can get, rather than to chase after what you want, but if you don't know what you want, I guarantee you'll be serving the agenda of those who do. That's how the world works. The 5% of people who know exactly what they want enlist the 95% who have no idea to help them get it done. If you're not clearly pursuing your own dreams and desires, the only other alternative is to be a slave to someone else's dreams and desires.

If you want to succeed in life and be fully alive, you've got to know what you want. You have to be crystal clear on what happiness and success mean to you. You've got to be ok to own your dreams and to chase desires, even though you may never get there. The moment you shut this down, you're squashing an integral part of your humanity. And that can't be good for you or the world.

95

Circle of Control – Influence – Concern

One of my favourite quotes from Henry David Thoreau is: 'I know of no more encouraging fact that the unquestionable ability of man to elevate his life by conscious endeavour.'

When it comes to becoming empowered to improve the quality of our life, it's useful to consider three areas of focus[27]:

1. The circle of control — the things we have 100% responsibility for and are totally in our capacity to change.

2. The circle of influence — the things we have some capacity to change and control.

3. The circle of concern — the things we worry about but ultimately have absolutely no capacity to control (like the weather, other people's opinions or choices).

4. The problem is that most people seem to spend all their effort in the circle of concern and get anxious and frustrated about things they have no ability to change. This then leaves them feeling disempowered and weakens their energy for true self-improvement.

The key is to let go and come back to focusing only on the things you have the direct capacity to control. We may not choose the things that happen to us, but we always get to choose our response. Reactive people find their circle of influence shrinks, while proactive people find that it increases.

96
Forgiveness

If you've ever been hurt, wronged, abused or taken advantage of in life, then you'll have faced the issue of whether or not to forgive.

It seems very common for people who've been in these situations to resolve inside that they'll *never* forgive. Yet, it turns out, that decision only ends up inflicting more pain and suffering on yourself.

Forgiveness is not about trust. It's about letting go of your right to hurt the other person back. This gracious act is a gift to your own soul and sets you free from being tied to that person and the situation any longer. When you hold unforgiveness as an attempt at punishing or hurting the offending party, it's like you chain yourself to them and the situation and therefore continue to give them the power to hurt you every day.

The amazing thing is that the person you hold unforgiveness towards often goes about their lives without remorse or consequence, and it's you who suffers instead. Your marriage, health and job all suffer because of the bitterness that starts to consume you from the inside out.

Forgiveness is a gift to yourself and an act of great strength, not weakness.

97
Letting Go of Labels

....

Sometimes our language restricts us from experiencing the wonder of the world we live in.

Labels can be helpful to categorise and simplify, yet they can also generalise and cause us to lose sight of the sheer magic and beauty in the world by making things commonplace and bland. If it's just a bird, just a tree, just a cloud, just a kid, just an old man, just a woman, then it's easy to walk on by, thinking there's nothing special to see.

But losing the label and just being present to what is, opens up a whole new world again. If you weren't allowed to use that language, what magic and beauty would you notice that was previously hidden under that label?

The moment you write anyone or anything off as just the label you use to describe them, your world becomes condensed into a very small and predictable place.

If you want to see the world in multidimensional, high-definition full colour, try being present and open to all that's around you by letting go of the labels.

98
Ramsey-style Honesty

I reckon we all need a bit of Gordon Ramsey treatment from time to time. Someone who has the balls to get up in our grill and tell us to wake up. Someone who is willing to shock us into seeing what we hide from or pretend not to know. Even someone who has no problem highlighting our mistakes, faults and weaknesses.

I got introduced to a friend of a friend the other day. Lovely guy — except he had a funky layer of plaque all over his front teeth. Now, who knows what's going on there, but chances are he isn't aware of how horrific it looks, nor the affect it has on others when meeting him for the first time.

Perhaps his mum never taught him about dental hygiene, but the bottom line is that someone needs to tell him to sort that out. Gordon Ramsey would. Sure, it would probably hurt his feelings at first, but I imagine he would eventually be grateful for the benefits of having a nice, clean smile.

Self-awareness is massively underrated. We all have blind spots, weaknesses and bad habits we think no one else can see, yet the fact is it's often the first and only thing people see. We all need to find people in our world who are bold enough to give the Gordon Ramsey treatment so we're confronted with reality and can sort that stuff out!

99
The Best Way Not to Get Hurt

One of my Facebook friends recently posted, 'The best way not to get hurt in relationships is to have no expectation of others.'

Really? This is the best way? To just be ok with whatever? However you treat me will be fine? I get what she was saying, but surely there's a better way to avoid the pain of others hurting you than to have no expectations of them.

What about the fact that we are each 100% responsible for training others how to treat us by what we allow and what we deny? I actually have very high expectations of how people will treat me. It's my job to teach them that if they'd like to be in my world, then they'll need to work out how to treat me well. If they don't, they won't last.

The golden rule is to love your neighbour as you love yourself. Great relationships always start with self-love. Owning the fact that we're valuable, worthy and deserving of love means we then treat others well and demand that they do the same for us. Don't lower your standards to avoid getting hurt. Make them higher!

100
The Long Haul

It's important to discover that you can't win or lose at life in any one moment or even in any one day. Realising this truth instantly takes the pressure off you needing to get it right all the time.

Parenting is a great example of this. You can't be a perfect parent. You can't always control your temper, always listen to your children, or always provide opportunities for them to be at their best. If you place these kinds of expectations on yourself, you'll live with constant anxiety that you're not doing enough.

On the other hand, great parents give themselves permission to be real. That means there will be mistakes, regrets and bad days. One of the things great parents do so well though, is what happens after these mistakes. They apologise, own their mistakes, take responsibility for the consequences and get themselves back in the game to do things better next time.

They realise they've probably got about 18 years to make a lasting impact on their kids before they fly the nest. They believe in their ability to have more good conversations than bad ones, make more good choices than poor ones, demonstrate love, care, compassion, generosity, integrity and kindness more often than not. Overall, they believe they'll be a blessing to their children and that the impact of their great parenting will last for generations.

This belief makes them a far better parent than those who have to get it right all the time.

101
Be Careful What You Wish For

Everything comes with a price. Exploring the consequence of achieving your dreams and desires is often the most neglected or overlooked part of the goal setting experience.

Take these goals for example — winning a gold medal at the next Olympics, earning $250k a year or getting a big promotion at work. They all sound incredible, and I'm sure they are, but they all come with a hefty price tag.

Winning gold may cost you every other area of your life. Gaining the promotion may mean having to neglect your family. Earning $250k could cost you by having to be at your best six days a week, rather than cruising through life only needing to perform for special occasions.

I'm not in any way trying to discourage you from chasing your dreams, just make sure you weigh up the cost of change against the cost of staying the same. Everything comes with a price. What if you gain the world, but lose your soul in the process? Will it be worth it?

You can have whatever you want as long as you're fully willing and able to pay *all* the associated costs.

102
Set up a Winning Week

When it comes to planning your life, it's important to work with the right chunk size. Trying to manage your life a day at a time can prove problematic. You'll end up overwhelmed with details and lost in endless 'to-do lists'. This chunk size is too small.

Planning your life a month or year at a time, on the other hand, is far too big. There's too much to focus on at once with too much shifting sand and unknown variables.

My suggestion is that a week is the perfect amount of time to play with.

Targeting a week at a time allows you to make great progress while staying highly flexible. Planning weekly allows you to make regular course corrections to stay on track.

Here are seven things to factor into your week to guarantee it will be a winner:

1. A meeting with yourself
2. A meeting with the key people in your life
3. A rhythm of rest
4. Nutrition and exercise
5. Investment in quality relationships
6. Life-giving rituals
7. Learning and development

If you get these seven things locked into your week ahead of time, it doesn't matter what else happens, you're guaranteed it will be a winning week.

103
Meeting with Yourself

....

The first part of setting up a winning week is to meet with yourself. For you to live a compelling and effective life, you'll need to be very good at being you. This will only happen as you learn to build an incredible relationship with yourself. Booking in a weekly meeting with yourself allows you to open the lines of communication between your body, mind, emotions, heart, head, soul, conscious and subconscious.

If you've never done this before, here's how to start.

1. Find a space that gives you access to a great mental and emotional state.

2. Grab a notebook, nice pen and coffee, along with your weekly planner or calendar.

3. Allow one hour of uninterrupted time, preferably on a Sunday evening or first thing Monday morning.

4. Having an effective meeting with yourself is all about checking in and asking great questions. It's also about listening and gaining new levels of awareness about where exactly you are now and where exactly you would like to be.

5. It requires you to take 100% responsibility for your current results and the results you would like to achieve. It's about giving yourself permission to flourish and investing in a high-quality relationship with the real you.

104
Meeting with Your Stakeholders

The second part of setting up a winning week is to make sure you schedule a strategic meeting with those you have skin in the game with.

Your stakeholders are your spouse, your kids, your colleagues, your staff and your business associates. The higher the quality of your communication with these important people, the better it is for everyone. Obviously, the nature of these meetings will be different depending on the stakeholder you're meeting with.

Your kids

You need to have a strategic meeting without them knowing it's a strategic meeting. It has to be casual, not forced, and may require a high level of creativity on your part. The point is, making time to actively listen to them and involve them in your decision-making as a family is super important.

Your spouse

This strategic meeting needs to be relational and conversational. If it feels like a committee meeting or a parliamentary sitting, both of you will avoid it. I think the best way to set up the space for weekly conversation is while doing something together. Walking, driving or eating all allow you to cover the key points while keeping it nice and relaxed.

Your work colleagues, partners, employees etc.

This strategic meeting needs to be clearly set up as such. Although you may also be friends with these people, the main function of your relationship is the shared work you're involved in. Therefore, make the meeting as clear and intentional as possible.

105
Developing a Rhythm of Rest

The third part of setting up a winning week is to ensure you factor rest into each day — more than just the six to eight hours of sleep you get at night.

Rest is one of my favourite aspects of an outstanding week. I think most people overlook the importance of rest. For this to work well, the key word is RHYTHM. If you try and cram all your rest into one day each week, you're totally missing the point.

Our body takes time to recover and rid itself of the chemicals produced when we're engaged in stressful, energy-zapping activities. The aim is to develop a rhythm of rest that brings the chemical balance back to zero every day, not just once a week. Trying to rest for only one day a week does not give your body long enough to come back to a neutral rest state.

The key is to be mindful of your energy levels throughout the day. To be at your best means there will be periods of high energy and full engagement, and periods of low energy and zero engagement. If you try and be 'on' all day, you end up running out of energy at crucial times anyway.

In your meeting with yourself, factor in some downtime each day and plug it in to your weekly planner. I have a full 90-minute nap scheduled for 2:30 pm every afternoon! While this may appear to be wasted time, it turns out that developing a rhythm of rest increases performance and efficiency.

106
Exercise and Nutrition

1. The fourth part of setting up a winning week is to intentionally factor quality nutrition and exercise into your schedule.

2. A recent study of Australian adults showed that 50% of our entire population has either a mental or chronic health issue — most of which are entirely preventable.

3. If you're going to win at life, you're going to need to be healthy. However, this framework is not about more discipline, effort and self-control. Rather, it's all about giving yourself permission to flourish.

4. The body craves health. It is home. It's the default position we come back to when we deal with all the doubts, fears and insecurities we're hiding behind. Have you given yourself permission to be beautiful, healthy, vibrant, successful and confident? Or are you self-sabotaging and hiding from the world to keep safe from being hurt, rejected or found out as inadequate?

5. There are three aspects for integrating health into your weekly schedule:

    a. Check in to see if you have permission to be attractive — if not, sort that out first.

    b. Plan exercise that you enjoy, with people you enjoy.

    c. Create a weekly meal plan and corresponding grocery list.

107
Investing in Key Relationships

The fifth part of setting up a winning week is making time to invest in key relationships.

What's the point of doing life well if you've got no one to share it with? We are relational beings who crave love and connection. I'm a big fan of social media and believe it opens up some incredible opportunities, yet one of the biggest challenges with our culture is that we end up being loosely connected to hundreds or even thousands of people at a surface level and then lose the art of connecting deeply to those around us.

I suggest you aim to have around 10 or 12 key people, not including your immediate family, who you walk alongside and share your life with.

The key is to be intentional about investing in these relationships, rather than just imagining they'll take care of themselves. These 10 or 12 people may be anywhere in the world, as long as you have the ability to keep in touch with them and grow your relationship.

Some things you might include in your weekly, monthly and annual planner are:

- having dinner together
- scheduling a phone catch up
- sharing food, coffee, beer
- exercising together
- planning adventures, and other things to look forward to
- sharing holidays.

108
Daily Rituals

The sixth part of setting up a winning week is scheduling daily rituals.

If you're going to succeed at life, you'll need daily rituals that help you get into a great state so that you're at your best when you need to be.

State is king. If you can control your state, you can control your outcomes. It's important to see that rituals are very different from disciplines. Rituals are life-giving practices that get you into a great state rather than disciplining yourself to do things that are good for you, but that you don't really want to do.

Rituals are very different for each person and can change over time. Some of my favourite rituals at the moment are:

1. cooking a creamy batch of porridge with my son on Friday mornings
2. going to the movies by myself every second Thursday
3. drinking peppermint tea in my rocking recliner after the kids have gone to sleep
4. reading fiction in bed before I go to sleep
5. morning journaling at my favourite coffee shop with my headphones in
6. joining the Tuesday morning bunch bike ride
7. doing an interval running session every Thursday morning.
8. The key is to get these into your calendar before the time mysteriously gets eaten up by a range of other things.

109
Learning and Development

The final part of setting up a winning week is making space for learning and development.

I'm amazed by how many people have no personal or professional development plan. Day in and day out they get up and do the same thing over and over. Successful people, on the other hand, are always developing themselves and are constantly learning ways to improve their results and the quality of their lives.

The thing about life is this — grow or die. If you're not moving forward, it's impossible to stand still. Whether you like it or not, the world is ever-changing and if you don't grow with it, you get left behind.

We live in an information age and have access to an abundance of resources for learning and development in any area we could imagine.

Therefore, when you map out your week, make sure you include time for some or all of these things:

1. self-improvement or personal development

2. career or work development

3. hobbies or personal interests

4. conversations with a coach, mentor or someone with permission to speak meaningfully into your reality.

110
Decisions

1. Every day we face an incredible number of decisions. Some choices are easy, and they don't really matter, while others are hard and the consequences are real.

2. I watch people find themselves at a crossroads with big decisions in front of them. Because they don't know what to do, or fear making the wrong decision, they make no decision at all. (No decision is still a decision, by the way.)

3. Often people become paralysed by the need to have 100% certainty about the outcome of their decision before they make it, but the truth is that there are no perfect decisions, only decisions. And, after each decision, there are more decisions! We can never fully know what's on the other side of the door. The only way to know for sure is to step through and find out.

4. Obviously, no one wants to make poor decisions as all our choices have implications for those around us, so in the face of uncertainty, here are three thoughts to help you make great decisions.

    a. When you don't know what to do, do what's right.

    b. When you don't know what's right, do what's in your heart.

    c. When you don't know what's in your heart, imagine you do.

111
Who Are You?

If you were to cut yourself in half to find yourself, where would you be? The life inside you, your soul or spirit, is not contained in any one part of you but is still inside you somewhere!

You're not your body, or your mind. You're not your possessions, achievements, roles, relationships or labels. You're not your behaviour, your choices or even the story you live out of. You're not your past and you're certainly not what others think or say about you.

So the question remains: Who are you?

The life that is in you is so wonderful, mysterious and sacred. You are someone uniquely valuable and special. This divine essence is demonstrated in your ability to create things that have never existed before. The limits of what you're capable of are all imaginary and only exist in your mind. Ultimately, you're exactly who you allow yourself to be.

Take a moment right now to stop, appreciate and acknowledge the wonder of what it means to be alive. Life is an extraordinary gift. What will you do with it today?

112
Language

The words we use don't just describe our reality, they shape it. Therefore, if you change the words you use, you change your experience.

Language is so powerful in determining how we feel about our life. One of my favourite rituals is to learn cool new words. If I find new language, then I can have new experiences opened up.

Here are some fantastic words I've discovered recently

5. Inexorable — unyielding and relentless

6. Obfuscation — to cloud or confuse the issue

7. Aesthete — one who cultivates great sensitivity to beauty

8. Nuance — the subtle variations that make all the difference

9. Ostensibly — appears or is stated to be true, though not necessarily so

Think about these words. What could you be inexorable about? In what ways are you playing games with yourself and others that keeps you disempowered? Where are you noticing beauty in the world? What micro-adjustments could you make that may create a massive difference?

Set yourself a goal of learning some cool new words this week to open up new experiences.

113
The Martyr Syndrome

A person's ability to survive in incredibly dysfunctional situations that they hate is truly extraordinary. One of the most powerful framing stories that keep people in these situations is the martyr syndrome.

In order to get to sleep at night, we all must square away with ourselves that we are decent human beings. We need to know that we're not a bad person.

One of the most common strategies we use subconsciously to make ourselves feel ok is comparison. If we keep ourselves surrounded by people who behave worse than us, then by comparison we're better than they are. Not only that but we also get extra brownie points for what we can tolerate while still functioning in the real world.

People in this situation almost need to be treated badly, so they can feel good about themselves. If they were surrounded by happy, healthy people they wouldn't have anyone to compare themselves to and would therefore have to question whether they were a good person again.

To break free from being the martyr, take 100% ownership of your own value and worth rather than needing to compare yourself to others.

114
Laziness

Did you know that laziness is never laziness? We're often quick to label ourselves, and others by our behaviour, but behaviour is always the fruit of something deeper.

If you were to observe a so-called lazy person 24 hours a day for a week, you would discover that this laziness is inconsistent. You would notice that they actually have lots of energy for some things and almost no energy for others.

Therefore, in getting to the bottom of things, it would be far more useful to explore the impact fear is having on their energy levels. It turns out the laziness is almost always a manifestation of fear. Fear paralyses and sucks energy from us more quickly than anything else.

If you're deeply afraid of failing or being rejected, then of course you're going to pull back from applying yourself in that area, so you don't get hurt. Therefore, if you want to change the amount of energy you have, you'll need to deal with the underlying fear first.

Using the laziness label is never true or useful. It only creates guilt and shame and never improves the situation.

115
The Fear of Success – Part 1

The fear of success is such a massive issue when it comes to people self-sabotaging their own goals. In order to understand how this subtle, yet powerful, fear operates, there are five aspects to explore. The fear of success is always about awareness, certainty, safety, state and story. Let's explore the awareness aspect first.

Because the concept of the fear of success is counter-intuitive, lots of people wouldn't even believe it's a thing. Yet, the surprising thing is that the fear of success is often a bigger hindrance than the fear of failure for most people. If you can't see it, or you don't believe it's a thing, the fear operates unchallenged and is free to do whatever it likes in your life.

1. When it comes to thinking about actually succeeding, the key is to see what you are specifically afraid of. This is made more real by success rather than failure.

2. For example, success may expose you to potential judgement, criticism or conflict. Or perhaps the fear is that once you've set a standard, you won't be able to sustain it.

3. The point is, in order to deal with the fear of success, you need turn the lights on and have a look at exactly what you're dealing with.

116
The Fear of Success – Part 2

The second aspect of the fear of success is certainty.

1. All humans crave a sense of order, control and safety. As Anthony Robbins says, certainty is one of our six core needs. One of the scariest things about success, on the other hand, is that it pushes out into the unknown. We all know how to fail because we do it so often! Failure is familiar and safe, yet success always pushes us into uncertainty, beyond comfort zones and into new and unknown experiences.

2. Success threatens our need for certainty.

3. The need for certainty has to be met one way or another, so in order to overcome the fear of success, it's essential to find resourceful ways of meeting the need for certainty that also allow you to go beyond your comfort zone.

4. The key is to let go of the need to control things that are ultimately out of our capacity to control and instead focus 100% on what we can control.

5. Overcoming the fear of success requires you to find certainty by embracing uncertainty and backing yourself! This means finding certainty within yourself rather than looking for it externally.

117
The Fear of Success — Part 3

The third aspect of the fear of success is that it's an issue of state management.

Your mental and emotional states totally affect the outcomes you produce in your life. Remember, state is king. Your state determines what you're capable of and what seems possible or impossible to you.

When you're in a great state, for example, you have access to your best ideas, creativity, intuition and magic. But when you're in a poor state, it's almost impossible to make good decisions, be creative or access energy and motivation. It turns out that the fear of success only surfaces when you're in a poor state.

If you're in a great state, fear and the associated self-sabotage totally disappear. This means that if you can control your state, you can also control this fear.

Let me remind you of the three quickest ways to manage your state:

1. Change your focus — fix your attention on positive things.

2. Change your physiology — breathe, stand tall, dress for success.

3. Change your language — use words, phrases and metaphors that are full of life, energy and positivity.

118
The Fear of Success – Part 4

The fourth aspect of the fear of success is safety. The problem with stepping into success is that it can threaten our desire to feel safe at the same time.

In order to give yourself permission to succeed, it has to be sustainable. You can't turn off your need for safety. Every cell is wired for self-preservation. To overcome the fear of success, therefore, success must also be safe.

Conversations about success and growth often create such a strong sense of positivity and unlock a world of new possibilities that sometimes the importance of safety is overlooked. Often people make passionate commitments to take massive action that is very high risk and unlikely to work out well.

One bad experience pursuing success like this can lead to a person developing a fear of success that stops them trying to be successful again.

The key is to weigh up the cost of success before you begin. Everything comes with a price. Having considered all the consequences, you can then choose a path that allows you to succeed without being exposed to undue risk at the same time.

119
The Fear of Success – Part 5

The fifth aspect of the fear of success is story.

We all need stories to live out of, yet some stories make you feel like success is somehow inappropriate, undeserved or a bad thing. These stories don't allow you to succeed.

For example, maybe it's your family story. Perhaps you had a rich uncle who was also arrogant, rude and selfish. He was always the example of what not to become. So, the thought of success is linked with the fear that money will ruin you.

Or perhaps it's the Aussie story. We are one of the only countries in the world that has the tall poppy syndrome. We love the battler and pride ourselves on our humility. Success would then make you arrogant.

Even some people's versions of religious stories can hold them back from success.

When it comes to your life, it's crucial to understand you're not the actor in the story you are living out of, you're the storyteller. Whatever your story, the key is to live out of a story that makes it ok to succeed, otherwise the fear of success will continue to hold you back for the rest of your life.

120
Letting Go of the Can

People often feel that the things causing them the most grief in life are holding onto them. The truth is often the other way around. They're the ones holding on to their dysfunction instead.

My favourite example of this comes from *The Simpsons*.[28]

On his way home from work, Homer ends up getting both hands stuck inside two vending machines while trying to steal the contents. In the next scene, the area is cordoned off and emergency services are there to attempt the rescue.

Fireman: Mr Simpson, there is no easy way to say this, we're going to have to saw your arms off.

Homer: But they'll grow back, right?

Fireman: Oh. Yeah.

Other Fireman: Ah — Homer, are you just holding onto the can?

Homer: Your point being?

What a powerful metaphor! We too, have the power to set ourselves free by letting go of the can. The moment we're done with being the victim in our story, we can let it go.

121
Real Generosity

It's common for people to list generosity as one of their core values. Yet what looks like generosity can actually be the act of being stolen from.

Generosity is at the hand of the giver, not the taker. If you can't say no and are constantly being taken advantage of, that's not being generous.

Often those with people-pleasing tendencies look similar to those who are generous, however, the big difference is the core motivation. One is focused on others while the other is worried about themselves.

People who can't say no are driven by the need to be liked and thought well of by others. When they say no, they feel guilty, so in order to sleep well at night, they keep saying yes.

True generosity looks like this:

1. Seek what is best for others out of a desire to serve.

2. Be prepared to say no when that's what is best.

3. Never operate out of obligation or the expectations of others.

4. Never get stolen from in terms of your time, money or relationships.

5. Give because you choose to, not because you have to.

6. Be willing to put your own oxygen mask on first before helping others with theirs.

122
Secrets to Great Relationships

A great marriage does not happen by accident. There are many ingredients that need to come together from both parties to produce such a rare treasure.

Here are five secrets couples with great marriages use to cultivate their romance.

1. They always deal with current issues until they're resolved. They never sweep issues under the rug or stack issues on top of issues.

2. They always negotiate like adults. They keep the standard of communication high and don't tolerate childish behaviour from each other.

3. They both position themselves as the prize. They each hold on to their individual value and worth, separate from their partner's.

4. They acknowledge that marriage is not based on a historical decision to say yes to each other, but on a daily decision to say yes. This means they're in the relationship because they want to be, not because they have to be.

5. They prioritise their own personal growth as a non-negotiable. They understand that their ability to give and receive love to each other flows out of the overflow of their willingness to deeply love themselves first.

123
Speaking into Someone Else's Reality

When I first learnt the coaching skillset, I was quite hazardous to those around me. In my enthusiasm to be helpful, I was far too eager to give advice. Equipped with wonderful new tools and insights into human behaviour, I was astounded by what I could now see in others' lives as well as my own.

Embarrassingly, my motto was that if I could see it, I was going to say it., and I'd clean up the mess later. Needless to say, there was quite a lot of a mess.

One of my great mates and fellow coach, Matt Waldron,[29] helped me understand the folly of my ways. He taught me there are only three conditions that make it ok to speak into someone else's reality.

1. As a parent of young children — however, the older the kids get, the less automatic right the parent has to speak into their world.

2. As a professional — when someone is directly paying for knowledge and advice.

3. If asked specifically — and when you're given explicit permission to do so.

At all other times, speaking into someone else's reality without direct permission is judgemental and presumptuous. As well-meaning as you may be, and even if you're 100% right, speaking into someone else's reality without permission is 100% wrong.

124
Hope is not a Plan and Sorry is not a Solution

Hope is an interesting word. It can be very meaningful and full of depth, yet I often hear people use it in a way that's actually very disempowering.

I hope things will work out, I hope things will improve, I hope I get the job, I hope my kids turn out ok, I hope my marriage survives — do you say these things? They all sound like you're saying plenty and that your words are full of intention, commitment and promise but in reality you're saying nothing. In fact, you may even be saying less than nothing, lulling yourself into a false sense of security.

Hope is not a plan.

And while we are at it — sorry is not a solution.

Sorry can be an easy word to roll out when you make a mistake or when others are upset with you, yet, again, it doesn't guarantee anything will change or that you'll behave any differently in the future.

Instead of using empty language, be crystal clear about both your plan and your solution. Don't leave things up to chance. Take 100% responsibility for what's happening and what you would like to happen.

125
Overcomplicating Issues

One of the best ways to avoid dealing with difficult issues, is to overcomplicate them in your mind.

It's an interesting strategy because while the solution may not be easy, the issue is never really that complex.

So, if overcomplicating our issues moves us further from the solution, why do people do it?

It turns out there are a number of great payoffs for making problems more complicated than they need to be. Here are a few of them:

1. You get pity from others when you explain your situation.

2. You don't have to face things if they're complicated.

3. You've got a great excuse for not solving the problem.

4. You feel important because of the drama and excitement the complicated problem adds to your life.

I've said it before, people often imagine the things that cause them the most grief in life are firmly holding onto them, when in fact the opposite is true. We're able to let go when we no longer need to hide behind our stuff.

The way out may not be easy, but it will definitely not be complicated either. Don't confuse simple with easy. The way out of dysfunction is always simple and hard.

126
Navigating Past Gatekeepers

Joseph Campbell's metaphor of the *Hero's Journey*[30] is one of my favourite coaching frameworks. One of the key ideas to come from this metaphor is the importance of navigating past the gatekeepers. A gatekeeper is someone in the hero's world who stands between them and the way into their real adventure. The gatekeeper often has good intentions of trying to keep the hero safe, but they also prevent the heroes from pursuing their destiny.

Sometimes, friends and family can be like gatekeepers in our lives. They make it hard for us to chase our dreams and constantly remind us of the dangers that lie ahead. Often, they're threatened by our dreams and want things to remain how they've always been. They try to convince us that if we move beyond them, we'll be all alone.

The gatekeeper has many tricks up their sleeve to prevent the hero moving beyond them. Emotional blackmail, historical obligation and the lie that if they proceed, they'll be all alone. Therefore, it takes great courage to embrace the call to adventure. When we do finally step out and follow our dreams, the heroes always discover they're not alone at all and that there are a whole bunch of new companions on the journey.

127
Stress

....

Did you know that stress is simply the perception of being under threat? This means that stress is an internal response to an external experience. Yet, what causes a stress response for one person, is a non-event for someone else.

The moment we perceive ourselves to be under threat, our nervous system kicks into gear and releases all the naturally-produced stress hormones to place us on high alert. Being under stress for a sustained period of time is obviously unhealthy. The chemicals that prepare us for battle are also poisonous to our bodies.

The key to experience less stress, therefore, isn't necessarily to try and remove yourself from external pressures, but to work on changing your internal perception of these experiences.

When faced with something difficult, the moment you tell yourself that you're not up to the challenge, the situation will be perceived as a threat. This means you're now officially under stress! If you face your limiting beliefs about yourself, however, and discover you're perfectly capable of handling any challenge, then your body will no longer produce the stress response in the same situation.

128
Energy and Rest

The law of conservation of energy[31] states that energy is neither created nor destroyed. It's simply transferred from one form to another.

This is very useful information to keep in mind when trying to motivate yourself to be at your best. Most people seem to believe they need to work more, sleep less and use more effort to get better results. Yet this strategy goes against the laws of physics.

You only have a certain amount of energy to live your life with. If you stay up all night working on a project, you've actually cashed in tomorrow's energy today. You can't then expect to have the energy to do that again the following evening. If you rob Peter to pay Paul, it eventually catches up with you.

Energy is like a bank account — you can't keep making withdrawals or eventually there will be nothing left.

Your body needs to draw energy from nutrition, rest and exercise to replenish your supply. Therefore, the key is to manage your energy, not your time, and stop messing with the physics.

129
Be Happy and Significant

As you can probably tell, I'm quite taken with the idea of happiness and success. I believe we're all capable of it, but few people will ever truly find it.

The quickest way to experience success, however, is to stop, be present and appreciate the beauty of what you already have. If you can't work out how to be happy and here, and if you can't see yourself as successful now, then chasing the dream will never satisfy you either.

Happiness is often a destination that always seems just out of reach. We keep telling ourselves we'll be happy when we get there or when we achieve our goals.

The problem is that if we tie our happiness to achieving things that are outside our control, then we've signed up for perpetual disappointment and unhappiness. Things very rarely work out the way we would like them to and no plan survives its collision with reality.

The key is to cut the cord that links your happiness to doing or having certain things and find how to be happy here. Now.

130
Modelling Success

The great thing about success is that it leaves clues.[32] The people who do well in any area of their life don't do so by accident. There are always key reasons why they have achieved the results they've got.

This is great news for the average punter. One definition of Neuro Linguistic Programming (NLP) is that it's the science of modelling excellence. It's all about deconstructing the exact strategy, beliefs and behaviour used by those who achieve excellent results for the purpose of replicating them.

So, for the areas you'd like to improve in, go and find the people who have better results than you, or have already produced the results you'd like to achieve. Then examine exactly what they do, think and believe differently from you. Now you can model them. If they can do it, so can you. Success is a science not a lottery.

There is absolutely no point recreating the wheel when plenty of people have gone before us and demonstrated the way to succeed.

131
Overthinking

Sometimes when I'm walking up the flight of stairs to my office, I find myself watching my feet do their work. Every time this happens, however, I immediately have to stop before I trip and fall.

I'm marvelling at how my feet are navigating these stairs so well without any deliberate input from my mind, yet the moment I start thinking about what comes naturally to me, things get really weird and stop working.

It got me wondering about how many other things I overthink, and as a result, mess with my own ability to get the job done. There's a lot to be said about trusting our subconscious to take care of the important tasks. We know how to breathe, walk, talk, drive, sit and sleep without consciously controlling the process, so what else should we be more inclined to trust our subconscious to take care of?

The role of intuition, gut response and instinct are often underrated in today's world. Overthinking can paralyse us. Sometimes the last thing we need to do is think!

132
Accountability

I train a lot of coaches who are really keen to get great results for the people they're working with. A common assumption is that one of the most useful things they can offer people looking for change is to hold them accountable for the actions they've committed to take.

I'm convinced that accountability is massively overrated. A friend of mine asked if I could hold him accountable to three key actions he needed to take. He wanted me to ask him about it every day for a month. He's a great mate, but there's no way I'd ever agree to a crazy plan like that. If he needs me to remind him about actions he wants to take, then the take-home point is he doesn't really want to do this after all.

Having someone hold you accountable to a course of action never brings lasting change. It's an external motivation source — as soon as it stops, so does the action you're taking because of it.

Lasting change is always driven from internal desire. Are you willing to take 100% responsibility for your own results rather than outsourcing them to someone else?

133
Nuance

State is king. If you can control your state, you can control your outcomes.

I've said before that one of the best ways to change your state is through life-giving rituals. Because rituals are so subjective — what can be great for one person's state can be terrible for another — it requires a great ability to listen to yourself to know the rituals that will work best.

One of my favourite words that helps with this idea is 'nuance' — which means subtle variation. When it comes to rituals and state, micro-adjustments and subtle variations really make a massive difference.

For example, I've discovered that I'm most relaxed not just in a comfy chair, but a comfy chair that rocks. It's not just a cup of tea before bed, it has to be peppermint. It's not just reading that helps me get to sleep but reading fiction. Eating plain crinkle cut potato chips after Cadbury's Dairy Milk chocolate really does it for me, but if I get the order around the wrong way — not so much.

How well do you know yourself and what gives you life? Take it to the next level by exploring the nuance around what really creates a great state for you.

134
Building Trust

Trust is one of the most essential elements to life. It affects every relationship we're part of. Without trust, it becomes impossible to walk alongside others.

Patrick Lencioni, in his fantastic book, *The Five Dysfunctions of a Team*,[32] says that every challenge within a team can be traced back to a lack of trust.

The key to building trust is through vulnerability. Remember the old team-building game where one blindfolded person has to fall backwards and trust the person waiting behind will catch them? If the blindfolded person isn't prepared to make themselves vulnerable and fall backwards, there's no point to the exercise.

The problem with being vulnerable is that it's dangerous! Making yourself vulnerable means you expose yourself to the risk of people letting you down. What if others don't do what they said they were going to do? Trust takes courage. If you want to move forward in any relationship, trust is essential. However, vulnerability is the thing that makes trust possible in the first place.

135
The Power of *'This'*

I love the simple meditation practice, from author Brian McLaren, centred around the word 'this'.[34] He says one of the biggest challenges in being grateful is the abundance of extraordinary things we have around us all the time. This leads to familiarity which causes us to miss the wonder of these things and then take them for granted.

The word 'this' helps us stop and notice the magic of the moment again.

Instead of taking breathing for granted, stop and pay attention to the wonder of *this* breath.

You drive past the same scenery every day. Instead, stop and experience all the grandeur you can see in *this* view.

Eating dinner every night with your family can just become something you do without thinking. Take a moment instead to experience *this* bite, *this* taste, *this* family, *this* house and *this* feeling.

Saying goodbye to your spouse before heading to work is second nature. The next time you do it, notice *this* kiss, *this* touch, *this* smell, this person and *this* day.

One of the simplest, yet most powerful, ways of changing your emotional state is to stop and be grateful. Using the word 'this' shows you exactly how much you have to be grateful for.

136
Story

A great way to explore the patterns of your life is to see yourself like a fictional character created within a movie or storybook. This allows you to examine the script written for you and make any necessary adjustments to it.

Do you realise you have the capacity to not only be a character in the story, but also the author of the book? You actually get to choose how the story goes!

Often people seem amazed at the stuff that keeps showing up in their life again and again. They go from one drama, problem and issue to the next without noticing it's all part of a repeating pattern. Therefore, it makes no sense to be surprised. Of course this stuff keeps happening. It's written into the script.

In order to become the script writer rather than just the actor, here are a few questions to consider.

1. What kind of character are you? What are the common patterns, themes and experiences of your character?

2. Who helped you write the script? Who taught you how to live, how to be happy and what success was?

3. How would you like your story to go instead?

4. To get different results, you'll need to live out of a different script and therefore write a new story.

137
Narcissism is Never Narcissism

Labels are judgements that define and imprison people around a certain behaviour. It makes people feel better about themselves to be able to write others off by labelling them a certain way. Narcissism is another classic label that isn't at all useful.

Narcissism is defined as excessive interest or admiration in oneself. It's seen as extreme selfishness. However, the moment that label is applied, the underlying cause of the behaviour can neither be understood nor changed.

The people who feel the need to constantly draw attention to themselves and always big-note themselves are actually the most insecure people around.

While they look overly confident, they're actually desperate for love, affirmation and attention from others because they have an incredibly low sense of self-worth. They've never developed an internal reference point for their significance, so they desperately crave it to be acknowledged externally instead.

This doesn't justify their poor behaviour but gives a reason for why they feel the need to dominate the space with their needs. The key to dealing with narcissistic behaviour, therefore, is for the underlying insecurity to be faced and overcome.

138
Peace Comes from Resolution

Peace is not the absence of conflict — it's the resolution of conflict. You don't get real peace unless you actually sort stuff out. This requires the courage to face up to life and deal with issues rather than sweeping them under the carpet to avoid conflict.

The difference between a peacekeeper and a peacemaker is massive. One does whatever is necessary to appease both sides to maintain the appearance of peace, whereas the other does whatever it takes to end the tension by fully resolving the conflict instead.

For example, many people view conflict in the home as something to be avoided at all costs. They assume that kids seeing their parents arguing is always a bad thing. However, the unwillingness to tackle difficult issues for the sake of superficial peace often does far more harm than good. Couples who keep the peace rather than make peace teach their children that honest feelings must always be supressed.

When peace only operates on the surface, the unresolved underlying issues fester and grow. This always leads to less peace where it matters most.

True peace, harmony and connectedness are always hard fought. It requires you to be a peacemaker rather than a peacekeeper.

139

The Game Isn't Over Until You Give Up

Whatever your position in life right now, and no matter what odds are stacked against you, you're always in the game if you still believe you are. Every passing moment is another chance to turn it all around, to make a comeback, to sort things out and to rise above those who think you're done or who are saying you can't.

In the history of the world, every single person who is admired and held up as an example of success, had to overcome more than their fair share of adversity, setbacks and naysayers. They had every opportunity to sit down, shut up, go home or give up. Yet they didn't allow the down times to define who they were or to hold them back. They picked themselves up, dusted themselves off, ignored the critics and got back in the game.

It's so easy to get discouraged and give up when things get hard, but your life is much more likely to be defined by the strength you found when things were tough, than anything you did in the good times. Maybe it's time for you to give yourself a pep talk, mount a comeback and get back in the game.

140
Front Foot or Back Foot Living

....

Every new day presents each of us with an abundance of interesting opportunities. The problem is that most people live on the back foot and aren't ready for what comes their way. Capitalising on life's opportunities requires you to be on the front foot instead.

Back foot living is all about:

1. waiting for life to happen and hoping things improve
2. needing conditions to be perfect before you step out
3. expecting others to give you opportunities and blaming them when they don't
4. not being clear about what you want
5. serving the agenda of what others want
6. being afraid of failure and worried about and what could go wrong.

Front foot living is all about:

7. proactively giving yourself every chance
8. saying yes and working out how later
9. believing there is no failure, only feedback
10. being clear about exactly what you want
11. picking yourself rather than waiting for others to pick you.
12. Which foot are you living on?

141
Top Five Happiness Tips

Happiness is one of my favourite topics. Here's some great research from the world of psychology about the top five tips to maintain a happy life.

1. Stay fit and healthy. It's hard to be happy if you're sick and tired. Exercise and nutrition play a massive part in how much we enjoy life.

2. Pause at the end of each day for a few minutes and reflect on three things that went well. Gratitude changes our focus, and focus changes our state.

3. Plan positive events into the future. Having things to look forward to is a wonderful feeling. Sometimes the anticipation of a holiday is better than the holiday itself.

4. Dedicate time to developing quality relationships. We are relational beings so when it comes to happiness, friendships are essential.

5. Don't be afraid of intermittent periods of unhappiness. You don't have to be bouncing off the wall all the time. It's unsustainable. Bad days are inevitable. You can't have mountaintops without valleys.

142
The Power of Metaphors

A metaphor is a language device that simply uses one thing to explain another. It paints a picture using words that connect a familiar idea with an experience that's hard to quantify.

Metaphors also serve as the bridge between our conscious and subconscious minds. They affect so much in our lives without us even realising. They form the structure to our experience and frame what we expect to happen. Remember, the language we use doesn't just describe our reality — it shapes it!

The problem here is that it's easy to be using disempowering metaphors without even realising. These metaphors then have a negative impact on your experience of life.

For example, if I say that I'm 'in over my head' to describe a new business venture, then I'll feel like I'm drowning every time I think about it.

'Getting the kids ready for school is a war zone.' No wonder everyone is so combative in the morning.

Stop and explore the metaphors you're using to make sense of your life. How well are they working for you? Could you improve on them?

143
Shiny Object Syndrome

Do you struggle with SOS — shiny object syndrome? Are you easily distracted by shiny new ideas? Are you constantly starting new things without ever finishing the things you were already working on?

SOS is the adult equivalent of a small child chasing after shiny objects. Once they get there and see what the object is, they immediately lose interest and start chasing the next thing. For entrepreneurs, the shiny new thing may be business objectives, marketing strategies, clients or even other business ventures.

Fortunately, SOS isn't a diagnosable affliction. It's a problem with how you think. If this is you, here are three ideas to solve this thinking problem:

1. 'Begin with the end in mind.' — I know of no greater course correction tool than this wisdom from Steven Covey. When you start each day with your eye on the prize, it's easy to weed out distractions.

2. Keep a list of all the things you're working on somewhere you can see it every day. It's easy to deceive yourself about how many new projects you're starting, and SOS thrives in the dark.

3. Celebrate finishing projects not starting them. Set enticing rewards ahead of time to link great pleasure with seeing things through to completion.

144
Influencing Others

I'm sure most people desire to have a positive influence on those around them. It's very natural to want to inspire and encourage others to do well and be seen as someone who helps people be at their best.

The problem is that most people often give advice to try and do this influencing, which proves to be the least effective strategy imaginable. To make matters worse, this advice has not been invited, and they are almost certainly not using their own advice on themselves first.

If you really want to help others around you grow and change, these are the three most effective ways of exerting positive influence instead of giving unsolicited advice:

1. Model what it looks like to live well and show the way. Demonstrate the power of your principles by showing how well they work in your own life.

2. Let go of what you want for others and tap into what they want for themselves instead. Internal motivation is always more powerful than external motivation.

3. Speak into their reality only when you're invited to do so. Even when you are given direct permission, tread carefully and avoid direct advice except when absolutely necessary.

145
Proving Your Worth

....

So much angst, frustration and dysfunction in life comes out of our own insecurity about trying to prove our worth to the world, or by trying to defend our ego in the face of perceived threats.

Basing your opinion of yourself on the approval and acceptance of others is a wonderful plan — until the moment someone disapproves of you and doesn't accept you. Then you're in a world of pain.

Yet, what if there was nothing to prove and nothing to defend? What if you were able to show up in the world, present and unguarded? I've said before that underneath every emotional, physical, relational and even financial issue is some kind of limiting belief about our own inadequacy.

We're desperate to feel loved and accepted but worry that we won't be. The key is to always take 100% ownership for your own value and worth as a human being rather than outsourcing that decision to your world, based on whether you can meet their expectations.

146
Friendships

Friendships give so much depth, colour and beauty to our lives. We're relational beings and don't cope in isolation. Having people in our world is essential.

However, no relationship is guaranteed to last forever. It's crucial not to cling to the historic nature of a relationship and recognise that friendships are all about seasons. Seasons change, and so do friendships. It's ok to allow people to come in and out of our lives, just as the seasons roll in and out. A particular person may bring so much life to you in one season, and then as you both grow and change, they can almost become toxic to you in the next season.

Giving yourself permission to let people go and move on with your life as the seasons change is a crucial aspect of doing life well. It's a really important piece of self-awareness to know when it's time to leave a relationship that's no longer healthy and not feel like you have to be friends for life.

The key is to notice when the effect of the people in your life moves from adding life to you, to taking life away from you. You have to go where the life is!

147
Learning to Fight Well

I find it amusing when couples pride themselves on the fact that they never argue. What they're actually saying is that one of them is dominant and used to getting their way all the time, while the other is passive and gives in easily to maintain the happy home.

The truth is that conflict is an essential part of healthy relationships and avoiding it is a recipe for growing apart. What's more, if two people agree on everything, then one of them is not necessary.

Seeing conflict is so important, it pays to get better at it. Here are three keys to learning how to fight well:

1. Set some ground rules before you have serious conversations. For example, one person talking at a time, talking like adults, taking responsibility rather than throwing blame and excuse.

2. Seek to understand, not just be understood. Putting yourself in the other person's shoes always helps to resolve issues more quickly.

3. Deal with issues as they arise. Never stack issues on top of issues.

148
The Clouded Mind

Here are three confronting but powerful questions to gain clarity when the way forward seems unclear:

1. How is it serving you to not have clarity?
The confronting reality is that there's nothing wrong with your mind. Not having clarity means you have a reason not to take action. The moment your mind is clear, the excuse is gone and now you have to do something.

2. What are you pretending not to know?
The truth of the situation is that it's likely you do know exactly what to do, or exactly what you're unclear about. Pretending not to know, however, means you can't be held responsible for this knowledge.

3. Is being super busy part of the problem?
When your life is so full of noise and activity, it's almost impossible to hear your own thoughts. Taking a weekend retreat, a day off, or a road trip to be still and quiet allows you to hear again. When you remove all unnecessary distractions, the way forward emerges very clearly.

149
Bright Spots

One of my favourite books about change is *Switch*, by Chip and Dan Heath.[35] They say that in times of change, you need a bright spot focus. That is, you need to look for what's already going right in your life, and then your mission is to study and clone it.

Our focus, in times of change, often goes instinctively to what's not working. We look for what's broken and then try to fix it. However, this approach doesn't always work very well. If we need to make major changes, then a lot of things are probably wrong, so it's hard to know where to even start.

Breakthrough happens when we look at the areas that are working in our lives and then apply what we learn about these bright spots to the areas that aren't working. We need to ask ourselves a question that sounds simple but is, in fact, deeply unnatural: What's working and how can we do more of it?

Instead of trying to work out why your kids keep failing mathematics, have a look at why they're killing it in English. Instead of obsessing over the work tasks you procrastinate about, become curious about the ones that energise and motivate you. Discover what's right, not what's wrong — then replicate it in the areas you are looking to change.

150
To Sell is Human

Author Dan Pink says that to sell is human. Whether we're employees pitching our colleagues a new idea, entrepreneurs enticing funders to invest, or parents and teachers cajoling children to study, we spend our days trying to move others. Like it or not, we're all in sales now.[36]

Many people have an inbuilt aversion to selling, but if you don't sell, then you're doing others a massive disservice because they have no opportunity to buy. To access the full value of your offering, others need to buy in. Just because you know how it's valuable doesn't guarantee others know that also.

This is why I never coach for free. A free session is of no use because the value has not been recognised, therefore the person being coached has no opportunity to value their own change journey.

The same is true for a free seminar you can go to, opposed to one you have to buy a ticket to attend. The content could be exactly the same, yet if it hasn't been sold to you then you can't access its true value.

So, to be successful at putting what you've got in the hands of those who need it most, you have to give people the opportunity to buy into what you've got. If they don't buy into it, they can't access the true value of it. If you put it out there without 'selling' it, then why would anyone listen?

151
Just Take Action

The world of social media is full of lightweight personal development advice that is really not that helpful. Here's something I saw recently — 'The only thing between you and your dreams is action.' Really? That's it? You mean I just need to try harder and do more stuff?

Sure, you've got to do some work to achieve your dreams, but saying that action is all that's between where you are now and where you want to be is like saying that to play at Wimbledon, all you need to do is hit lots of tennis balls. That's so unhelpful. I'll guarantee Roger Federer has done more than take action to be one of the all-time great tennis players.

It's not just action that will work — it's the right action, done the right way, all preceded with very specific beliefs about who you are as a person.

Rather than starting with what you need to DO, people who actually achieve their dreams work out who they need to BE to have access to those dreams in the first place. DOing always flows out of BEing.

Before you start taking more action and doing more work, take some time to align yourself to a successful way of BEing first.

152
Flow State

Russian flow state expert, Mihaly Csikszentmihalyi, explains that humans are at their absolute best when they operate from a place of high risk and high skill at the same time.

He describes the relationship between skill and risk like this:

1. High Risk + Zero Skill = Total Anxiety

2. High Risk + Medium Skill = Confidence

3. High Skill + Zero Risk = Boredom

4. High Skill + Medium Risk = Arousal

Obviously both boredom and anxiety are undesirable, but it's confidence and arousal that are most dangerous to human performance. Being in a high-risk situation where you don't quite have the skills to sustain, can easily lead to burnout or adrenal fatigue. Whereas operating from a safe place of 100% confidence looks amazing to others, but only produces good results not great ones.

The magic happens outside the safe zone. High risk, high skill. This is where we have our most meaningful and effective experiences and truly enter flow state.

To do your best work and make a meaningful contribution to the world requires you to develop your craft tirelessly but also be willing to step out of your comfort zone. If you don't put yourself in a position where failure is a real possibility, then true success isn't an option either.

153
Parkinson's Law

Parkinson's Law[37] states that work expands to fill the time available for its completion.

That means a task will take however long you give yourself to finish it. If you allow three months to finish that Uni assignment, you'll send if off at 11 pm the night before it's due. If you tell someone you'll get back to them within a fortnight, again you'll finish your response at the last moment.

I'm sure we all experience this law in action almost every day. Interestingly, this law also applies to money and food. That means your appetite expands to the amount of food on your plate and expenses expand to the amount of available income. Using a bigger plate means you eat more food and earning more money leads to spending more.

Therefore, the key is to set arbitrary deadlines and create restrictions on your time, plate size and available income.

For example, one of my favourite productivity hacks is to set an hourglass beside my desk to create an hour of power. One hour. Full gas. Then I must stop. This ensures my work cannot expand any further. By utilising Parkinson's Law in my favour, I achieve things within that hour that otherwise would take me all week or even longer.

154
Applaud Failure

Some time ago, I kept track of the number of big ideas I had for business growth throughout the year. After the first quarter, I'd tried at least 10 things that had all failed! I thought each idea was a good one, yet none of them worked out how I'd hoped.

One of my very favourite Nelson Mandela quotes is 'I never lose. I either win or I learn'. The cool thing about this is that it means I've moved incrementally closer to really achieving the things I dream of. Every failed attempt is a chance to learn something new, and every time I learn something it gives me more depth, wisdom and experience to get me where I want to go.

Sir Ken Robinson, in his popular 2006 TED talk,[38] says that if you're not willing to be wrong, you cannot create anything original. This means that without room for failure, creativity is impossible.

He goes on to say that for most of us the problem is not that we aim too high and fail, it's that we aim too low and succeed.

So come on, have a go. Stick your neck out. Make mistakes. Be ok with mess. The world needs your unique contribution. If you give up now, we'll all miss out.

When you're nearing the end of your life, will you be more disappointed with the things you tried and failed at, or the stuff you never even tried? Start applauding your failures. They're the things moving you closer to your goals more than anything else.

155
Are You Lying to Yourself?

No one wants to be labelled a liar. Lying to those around you is a serious offence, but what if lying to yourself could, in fact, be worse?

Do any of these things describe you?

1. Always deferring to the wisdom of others
2. Swayed by the loudest opinion
3. Mask, medicate and avoid emotional and physical pain
4. No original thought or idea in a long time
5. Don't know what you want anymore
6. Keep procrastinating about key tasks and putting off important decisions
7. Say, 'I don't know' a lot
8. Trying to be positive about everything
9. Haven't openly disagreed with someone in ages

These are great indicators that you're suppressing the best of you and lying to yourself about how happy, healthy and fulfilled you really are. The thing is that this lying eventually hurts you big time.

Turning off your honest response to life causes significant physical and emotional pain in your life and ultimately leads to trauma. Being willing to be truthful can be difficult and costly but, in the long run, honesty is always the best policy.

156
The Importance of Desire

While asking yourself the 'What do you want?' question is always dangerous and difficult, there's no denying it's the adult question and, as such, is still the most important thing we could ever explore.

Sure, it opens up the chance for conflict, judgement, responsibility, failure, disappointment, stress and mistakes — yet it also gives you access to a range of extraordinary gifts and possibilities.

Here's what can happen when you give yourself permission to keep asking this question:

1. You can improve the quality of your relationships, finances and health.

2. You can attract higher quality people into your life who allow you to be you, rather than keeping you small.

3. You can develop as a human being and reach your potential.

4. You can learn so much about yourself and who you really are.

5. You can inspire others to live large and chase their dreams too.

6. You can contribute your unique gifts and talents to the world.

7. You can move beyond merely surviving and start thriving.

So, what are you waiting for? Take some time out for yourself today. Grab your journal and a nice pen and give yourself permission to dream again.

157
Joy

I have honestly experienced more joy in my life in the last few years than in all the previous years combined. I've discovered that you can't just choose to be more joyful, but that joy shows up as the fruit from a range of other significant life decisions.

Here's what I've learnt about life that has given me true joy:

1. It's essential to be ok with highs and lows. If I flat-line through life, I may avoid the dark valleys, but I also rule out the mountain peaks.

2. Constant willingness to face up to life and find myself means, more than ever before, that the real me and the ideal me are one and the same. This personal congruence means I'm actually living in line with my values.

3. Being grateful for what's happened and what will happen always changes the point of focus from lack to abundance.

4. Looking back and seeing all the small steps in the right direction have led me somewhere cool. Progress always feels great.

5. Developing deep relationships with great people is a source of real life and love.

6. Being secure in my identity allows me to show up present and unguarded — from that place, magic always happens.

7. It's important to cultivate more sensitivity to beauty. When you stop and smell the roses, the world truly is a beautiful place.

Is experiencing more joy in your life important to you too? If so, what seed do you need to start sowing?

158
Find Your Gold

There are two basic options when it comes to the idea of self-improvement. You can focus on your weaknesses or focus on your strengths. Option one suggests we should work hard improving the things we're not good at, whereas option two directs all effort towards mastering the things we're already good at.

Both ideas certainly have their merit, yet as business guru, Jim Collins, says, good is the biggest enemy of great. In other words, the best that option one can give you is to become a generalist whereas option two only gives you the chance to become outstanding at one main thing.

Now this requires the security to be ok with doing some things poorly, and to be comfortable with the fact that you can't be good at everything.

I'm not sure that anyone really cares if LeBron James is any good at cooking or if John Mayer can run fast. But when they bring their A-game to what they do best, it's pure gold. When someone devotes their life to mastering their craft, the whole world benefits.

So many people undervalue what they are and overvalue what they're not. Get clear about the gold in you and focus on bringing the best version of that to the world.

159
Success is a Science

One of my favourite lessons about success comes from author and marketing expert, Siimon Reynolds. He says that success is a science. No matter what field successful people excel in, they've performed in a certain way and thought in a similar manner.[39] True success has nothing to do with luck, talent or even deservedness.

Here are a few of the predicable things successful people always do.

- They always have a clear sense of purpose for their life and are very clear about what they want. The average person is average because they don't know where they're heading. Without purpose, you're more at risk of becoming the outcome of somebody else's purpose.

- They always ask high-quality questions that lead them into new levels of awareness and growth. Most people ask low-quality questions that only ever keep them stuck and disempowered.

- They always utilise great daily rituals that help them get into a high-performance state. Rituals for sports people are common, expected and practised. Yet rituals for a successful life are much rarer and often overlooked.

The great thing is that if success is a science, then the process can be replicated for anyone.

160
Courage

Courage is not the absence of fear, it's the ability to feel the fear and act anyway. It really is ok to be afraid. I get scared all the time. Courage is all about realising what's important in life and aligning your actions with these things, rather than focusing on the fear and aligning your actions with that.

Fear is part of our self-preservation instinct. It reminds us we are alive and valuable and need to be protected from potential danger. If we felt no fear, something would be severely wrong. Don't judge yourself for being afraid, instead be grateful for the opportunity to step out and grow.

Every challenge provides you with an opportunity to overcome. It's through overcoming these challenges that we become stronger and our capacity is enlarged. If everything were safe, easy and risk free, there would be no value in any achievement, and we would never experience the joy of winning in life.

The things that provide us with the most meaning and fulfilment in life are always outside our comfort zone. You can't experience any of these things without a measure of courage.

The point is, fear is not evidence of you doing something wrong, it's just letting you know you're at the edge of what is safe, known and comfortable. The question is: What is beyond this edge?

161
Go Where the Life Is

I find it interesting that there are so many different and often opposing theories about the best way to achieve health and wellbeing. High fat, low fat, no carbs, no sugar, no wheat, high protein, dairy free, paleo, vegan — the list goes on. At the risk of being labelled a heretic, I'm not sure if the perfect diet actually exists, nor if getting diet 100% right is that important for overall health.

I consider myself to be very healthy, but most days I have some chocolate, cheese, blueberry yoghurt, plain crinkle cut chips and beer. I can't get enough of these basic staples! Sure, I also drink plenty of water, do lots of exercise and eat my fruit and veg, but I enjoy my life and I certainly enjoy eating delicious snacks.

Amazingly, it's been proven that your body processes calories differently depending on whether you eat with guilt or gladness.[40]

I have friends who are incredibly disciplined and place great restrictions on their diet, but I'm not convinced it's adding any real value to their lives. What is the point of adding extra years to your life if you're not enjoying the ones you've already got? Life is for living. When you give yourself permission to flourish in life, your body craves health. And you don't have to flog yourself to get it.

162
Ego

Did you know that it's our ego that separates us from life? Ego is us at our worst. It makes us selfish, needy and isolated. It keeps us disconnected from ourselves, others, the planet and God.

There are seven main ways our ego keeps us disconnected by causing us to focus on our false self.

1. I am what I have. I'm diminished by what I don't have. My possessions define me.

2. I am what I do. There's always more to be done. My achievements define me.

3. I am what I think. My thoughts control and define me.

4. I am what others think of me. My reputation defines me.

5. I am separate from everyone. My body defines me as alone.

6. I am separate from all that's missing in my life. My reality is disconnected from my desires.

7. I am separate from God. I'm lost and alone.

Yet, as Deepak Chopra says, to manage the ego, you need to live your life consciously because a conscious person makes better choices than an unconscious person.

This means being aware of your choices and why you're making them. The moment you're aware of your ego behaving like this, it gives you the chance to let go of the illusion of separation and become connected to life again.

163
Spiral Dynamics

One of the most profound and life-changing concepts I've learnt in the last 10 years is the theory of spiral dynamics[41], first developed by Dr Clare W Graves[42] and published by Chris Cowan and Don Beck.

They suggest that there are seven levels of development we can grow through as human beings. It's such a rich and deep model of human behaviour, so, at the risk of oversimplifying their work, here is my summary.

The levels are Survival, Tribe, Rebellion, System, Entrepreneur, Contribution, Statesmanship. These levels spiral between individual or collective levels of consciousness.

We're capable of living on one level in a certain area of life, and an entirely different level in another area. All seven levels are vitally important to living a meaningful life and it's impossible to skip or bypass levels that you don't like.

The key is to learn the lesson of each level so that we're able to keep growing and really reach our potential, rather than get stuck and stay on any one level.

I'll explain all seven levels in more detail in the following segments.

164
Moving Beyond Survival

Level 1 of The Spiral Dynamics is Survival. The whole focus of this level is simply on existing. How do I make it through to the end of the day without dying physically, emotionally, mentally or spiritually? All energy is taken up working out how to survive and, therefore, there's no energy being directed towards growth.

Survival is where we begin our journey. A baby is not thinking about their career, or who they'll marry. Their consciousness is consumed with how to stay alive.

There are certain times in life where we might find ourselves back in survival mode — where you're facing some massive challenges or struggles.

In order to grow beyond this level means finding a support network to belong to, thereby increasing your chances of survival. The key question is: Who can I depend on to keep me safe? You need some good people in your world as soon as possible. Left alone, you're in serious trouble.

165
Moving Beyond Tribe

Level 2 of The Spiral Dynamics is Tribe. The focus of this level is on rituals, culture, family bonds and working out who you belong to. Who are my people?

This is often a very superstitious level, steeped in long-held traditions passed down through the generations. Individuality has no place in this level, and you're not rewarded for independent thought or behaviour. Level 2 is instead all about living by the rules, traditions and culture of the tribe you're part of without question, because doing so keeps you very safe.

The key to making it beyond this level is taking responsibility for your own life and stepping into independence, even where it's against the beliefs or wishes of your tribe. Just because it's been done this way in your cultural group or family for generations doesn't mean it must go on this way. As stated, there's no space for this thinking within the tribe. Finding your own voice will see you ostracised and cast out.

However, to keep growing as a person means that, at some point, you'll need to rebel from the tribe — no matter what the cost.

166
Moving Beyond Rebellion

Level 3 of The Spiral Dynamics is Rebellion. This level focuses on defining yourself by what you stand against and what you don't agree with. This is about having a cause or a fight that consumes your energy and gives your life purpose. This level puts you at odds with the tribe and leaves you isolated from the support of others.

Although it may be perceived as a negative level, the level of rebellion is crucial for our development and teaches us very important lessons about who we are and what we're capable of. It also helps break off our need for approval from others and develop our own rules and ideas.

To stop at this level of growth, however, stunts your development as a mature adult. It renders you somewhat of a misfit, conspiracy theorist who is often angry at the world and unable to flow with others.

The key learning that allows one to pass beyond this level and keep growing is being able to fit in and function as a mature adult in the world. It's about learning to submit to authority, to trust and respect and play by the rules.

167
Moving Beyond the System

....

Level 4 of The Spiral Dynamics is the System. To grow from the level of rebellion to fitting into the system is a huge step. However, eventually the rebel realises that they're not getting anywhere on their own and not everyone is out to ruin their life. They realise it's time to cut their hair, get a day job and trust the wisdom of those who've gone before them.

This level is all about living as a responsible adult, playing by the rules and respecting the systems of authority around you. This is the level of stability, order, certainty and trust.

Like any of the levels of consciousness, the longer you stay, the unhealthier it becomes. So many people never grow beyond the safety of the system. People buy into the lie that they're weaker than they think and need to rely on others to make life work for them. This also causes them to lie to themselves about how happy and fulfilled they really are as they serve the agenda of others while saving for their retirement.

The key to move beyond this level is being willing to embrace risk, uncertainty and adventure. It's about entertaining the most dangerous and powerful question we face as human beings: What do you want? It's about finding your purpose in life and being willing to back yourself to make it happen.

168
Moving Beyond Entrepreneurship

Level 5 of The Spiral Dynamics is Entrepreneurship. This level focuses on innovation, pioneering creativity, business and financial abundance and thinking outside of the box. It's about opportunity, success, achievement and autonomy. To move into this level requires you to be willing to find your voice and speak your message.

Right and wrong become far less clearly defined and rules for what a person should do, think and believe are left behind. This level of consciousness allows you to move beyond exchanging time for money to leveraging your income by creating products and service.

The key to go beyond this level is to shift the focus from building your own empire to genuinely serving others. If you stay on Level 5, it becomes all about you, and you end up locking people below you in Level four. You need slaves or servants to do your thing without asking questions. You get threatened by people leaving to do their own thing.

To keep growing as a human, you need to learn to genuinely empower and add value to those around you without needing to get something in return.

169
Moving Beyond Contribution

Level 6 of The Spiral Dynamics is Contribution. This stage requires you to grow beyond entrepreneurship and your quest to do your own thing, and shift to seeing yourself as part of the global community. This is all about giving back, making a difference, philanthropic work and solving the major issues of inequality and injustice in the world.

Interestingly, I frequently talk to good people who are deeply motivated to make a huge contribution to the world but are still operating at Levels 1 through to 4 in their consciousness. They're very much resistant to the idea that they'll need to grow through all the levels to really be able to contribute. The problem is that they're banging their head on the lack of resources and limited thinking and never get to make a difference for more than a handful of people in their immediate circle.

Whether you like it or not, if you really want to make a difference in the world, you can't skip levels without learning the lesson each level provides.

So many people are afraid of money, business and stepping out on their own but the lessons you learn in Level 5 Entrepreneurship are ultimately what grow your capacity to genuinely make a difference to the world.

170
Growth Through Experience

In 2016, I moved my family to Germany for nine months as a business experiment to see if I could do what I do best from anywhere in the world. It was a big risk, but a great adventure.

Here are the top three things I learnt from my first week in Deutschland.

1. There's ALWAYS more need for growth. Getting on the plane, I felt like I was totally on top of my game. Yet once I left Australia, I discovered plenty of hidden limiting beliefs I didn't even know existed. The more I know, the more I realise I have yet to know.

2. State is king. Really it is. The state I'm in determines the outcomes I get. There is zero point operating out of a poor state. It's better to spend three hours managing my state, if that's what it takes, than spend those three hours struggling through work stuff. State management rituals often need to be updated too. What was working for me in Australia didn't suit me well in Germany.

3. The importance of surrender. I had to let go of the myth of control. I was in a foreign country where I knew so little. My ego would have me believe I'm isolated and alone, whereas surrender allows me to be open and connected to the source of all life, love, creativity and abundance.

171
Dirty Emotions

....

To be human is to be emotional. Emotions aren't good or bad, or right or wrong, they're simply an expression of being alive.

I learnt a new term recently, which has enabled me to have a more authentic experience as an emotional being. The term 'dirty emotions' refers to the secondary emotion we experience as a self-judgement of the first emotion.

For example, you may be feeling frustrated about something, but then feel disappointed that you're frustrated. Or you're upset about how someone has treated you, but then you feel guilty about feeling upset. You feel flat, but then hate that you've got no energy. I'm sure you get the point.

What if, instead, you were to give yourself the gift of allowing the primary emotional experience, without clouding it with the dirty secondary emotion?

When you remove the judgement, it allows you to process the primary emotion in a far healthier manner.

172
Decluttering

There's something incredibly therapeutic about decluttering your life. Whether it's cleaning out your wardrobe, garage, office desk or inbox, it feels great to get rid of things you don't need.

So why is that? It turns out we very readily attach our identity to our things. We subconsciously imagine that parting with possessions feels like losing part of our soul.

This, of course, is a low-quality attempt from our ego to prove our value and worth in the world. It's to attach our value and worth to what we do and what we have, instead of who we are.

We actually need far less than we keep. Letting things flow in and out of our lives, rather than desperately clinging to them, frees us from the addiction to stuff. It allows us to be more grateful, generous and at peace with our world.

Things can never really satisfy, nor could they ever define who we are. Intuitively, we know this is true, and the act of simplifying our life works to align us with this truth.

173
Gratitude in Advance

It's easy to be thankful for the good things that have already happened in your life, but to be grateful for the good things that are yet to happen is something else altogether.

Neale Donald Walsch says that gratitude in advance is the most powerful creative force in the universe.[43]

People fear that things won't work out because they haven't worked out before. As long as you believe your history is going to dictate your present and your future — it will.

The key to create a new program for your life is to be grateful for what you want to happen as though it *already has* happened. This changes your focus and expectation and ultimately your results. Practising gratitude in advance allows you to live as if the blessing you desire is a certainty!

Gratitude in advance is different from hope or wishing. It's confidence, belief and expectation. It's an ability to go into your own future and see things the way you'd like them to be rather than worrying that you'll end up with everything you don't want.

174
The Curse of Knowledge

Have you realised that sometimes the more you know about a subject, the harder it is for you to teach that knowledge to others? The term 'curse of knowledge'[44] was developed by three economists in the early 90s to explain this phenomenon. Once we know something, we find it hard to imagine what it was like not to know it.

You overestimate how much people understand you. It's that simple. You're suffering from the curse of knowledge when you know things that the other person doesn't and you've forgotten what it's like to not have this knowledge.

This makes it harder for you to identify with the other person's situation and explain things in a manner that's easily understandable to someone who's a novice. This is why 3rd-year university students often make better tutors than the professors. They can clearly remember how hard it was in their first year, while the professors have long forgotten.

The key to overcome this challenge is to simplify things far more than you think is necessary. Slow it down. Tell stories. Remember what it was like before you knew what you knew. Make sure you explain ALL the key steps in your journey that got you to where you are today.

175
High- and Low-Quality Problems

There's a big difference between high-quality and low-quality problems in life. A low-quality problem may be in your life because of poor choices. For example, 'I've got no money because I have a gambling issue.'

On the other hand, you get high-quality problems as the result of great choices. For example, 'I've got no money because I've finally backed myself in starting my own business and I've invested every last cent!'

The aim of the game is not to live without problems, but to be the kind of person who overcomes present challenges so you can earn higher quality ones. Here are some tips:

1. Expect to have problems in life. It's a natural part of growing as a human. As Franklin D Roosevelt famously said: 'Smooth seas never produce skilled sailors'.

2. Stop and review the problems you're currently experiencing. If they are there due to some great choices, celebrate your progress. If they are there due to some poor choices, learn from your mistakes and let the situation give you valuable experience.

3. Keep developing your capacity as a person so that you're constantly earning higher quality problems.

176
Life is not Fair

One of the most difficult but important life lessons I've worked my way through is the fact that life is not fair. Bad things happen to good people every day. The sooner you come to terms with this reality, the better it will be for you, otherwise you could end up spending the rest of your life feeling sorry for yourself over the cards you've been dealt.

Are you waiting and hoping things will somehow improve just because you feel you deserve something better? Just because you need something doesn't mean you'll get it. Just because you hope for something doesn't mean it will work out. Just because you try hard, doesn't mean you'll succeed.

Life responds to intention not injustice. You've got to know exactly what you want and what you're prepared to do to get it. That means showing up with desire, commitment, creativity, resourcefulness, flexibility, resilience and inexorability. You've got to be willing to adapt, grow and change to become the kind of person who has access to the kind of results you truly want — without giving up.

Life is not fair. So, what are you going to do about it?

177
Romance

It seems that one of the first things to disappear in any long-term romantic relationship is the sense of romance itself! I'm sure it's never the intention when two people start out together, but it's often where they end up.

Here are some simple but effective ways to rekindle the romance with your spouse.

1. Date once a week — It doesn't have to be anything fancy. No matter how busy or tired you are, just make some time for each other — kid free.

2. Smell good — A great smelling perfume or cologne has an incredible impact on the brain, which then filters through to the rest of our body.

3. Learn something together — Create exciting experiences you'll remember forever.

4. Send messages — Send a message for no reason other than to say you're thinking about your spouse.

5. Say new things to each other — If you're still only complimenting your partner on their nice backside 10 years into the relationship, that's not going to cut it.

6. Develop yourself as a person — Neediness and insecurity are the most unattractive things in any relationship.

178
Parents

Here's a question for all parents: At what point is it ok to transfer your energy away from chasing your own dreams to helping your kids chase theirs?

Think about the process of becoming an adult. It's about realising that you have to work out what you're going to do with your life and that your parents aren't always going to be around to do everything for you.

So, you go to university, pick a career, get a job and aim for the stars. But then real life sets in and you get scared and wonder if you have what it takes to really succeed in life. Next thing, you're married with your own kids, telling them to chase their dreams and that they can be as successful as they want to be.

Parents then get invested in their kids' goals as a way of finding meaning in their own lives because chasing their goals got too hard. The problem is that your kids see the hypocrisy of it all, just as you did with your parents.

The best and only way to empower your kids to chase their dreams is to model what it looks like and show them that it's possible. Never give up on your own life to help someone else with theirs. It just doesn't work.

179
Energy

I'm still amazed at what happens in my body simply based on what I've focused my attention on. When you're having a bad day and feeling really flat, it certainly doesn't feel like you're choosing that experience, yet, while you didn't choose the feeling, you did choose what to focus on.

Mulling over the negative things in your life will suck the energy out of you, every single time. Just as focusing on what's great will fill you with life and energy every time.

If you want more energy, focus on what is going well for you, who you love and what you're grateful for. If you want to feel flat, focus on people who don't get you, stuff that hasn't worked out yet and what you're afraid of.

So, before you tell yourself a story that your energy levels are outside your control, take a moment to notice what you're focusing your attention on. If you're feeling flat right now you can change it or, if you like, you can enjoy your bad day instead.

180
The Karpman Drama Triangle

Dr Stephen Karpman suggests that in interpersonal conflict there are three main roles that get played out. He calls this interplay of characters the 'drama triangle'.[45]

The persecutor: also known as the bully or villain. They are the bad guy in the story making everyone else's life difficult. The persecutor always requires a victim to torment. The persecutor gets to feel significant by having power over others.

The victim: the one getting treated poorly all the time. They feel hard done by, powerless and weak. The payoff, however, is that the victim gets to feel pity by being treated badly by others, and things are never their fault. In order to remain the victim, they always need a persecutor in their life, but also a rescuer.

The rescuer: the hero in the story. They always need to save people from their problems in order to feel good about themselves. By constantly rescuing people, however, they actually disempower the victim and keep them in their story. Rescuers need victims and persecutors to keep the drama working.

To change this dysfunctional cycle all it takes is one part to stop playing their role. If one part of the triangle ceases to play along then the drama collapses. If this happens, the persecutor can become a Challenger, the victim can become a Survivor, and the rescuer can become a Coach.

181
All Alone in the World

One of the worst tricks our ego plays on us is leading us to believe we're all alone in the world and, therefore, we're threatened, lonely, insecure and unloved. This leaves us always feeling separated from God, the planet, each other and even from ourselves.

However, this is purely an illusion. You and I are actually deeply connected to, and deeply dependent on, the life all around us. Everything is connected, and everything is spiritual. Even the atoms that are building blocks of all matter are atoms, comprised almost entirely of energy.[46] The sun, the moon, trees, plants, clouds, earth, wind, fire, animals and people are all sharing this life together. They're all dependent on each other and all operating in the same system.

How could we ever imagine we're alone and unconnected? Opening up to life and letting go of the illusion of separation actually connects you to beauty, creativity, love, kindness, receptivity, abundance and expansion. These things are what hold the universe together and aligning ourselves with them always allows us to experience life to the full.

You could never be alone in the world no matter how hard you try.

182
Get Your Power Back

In order to take your power back, you have to be willing to let go of the payoff you got for giving it away in the first place.

Lots of people feel incredibly disempowered in life and that they've had their power taken away from them. Yet, interestingly, personal power can never be stolen — it's only ever given away. And the only reason we'd give it away is if we got something valuable in return.

This is confronting, I know, but incredibly liberating at the same time because it means we're not victims. We're exactly where we've chosen to be. Which means we could also make different choices.

The main payoff for giving away your power is that, by doing so, we get a measure of protection from the things we're most afraid of. Blame and excuse is far easier than embracing responsibility and choice. We get to play the victim and hide so as to never get found out, examined or exposed.

If you're willing to face the underlying insecurity, you can let go of these things and take your power back today.

183
Listen to Your Dreams

Lasting change in our life is always internally driven. External motivation may provide short-term change, but it's never sustainable. Real change comes out of the deepest, strongest and best part of us, longing for more. This part is often hidden, ignored and undervalued and only comes out when we're prepared to listen.

If you want to know what's going on beneath the surface in your life, listen to your dreams. This is often one of the best ways to understand your deep fears and deep desires. When we're asleep, our controlling conscious mind is out of the way, and our subconscious is free to play. Dreams are where your subconscious warns you, teaches you and gives you vital keys to make the best decisions for you.

Don't get too caught up with dream interpretation books or experts. Your dreams can only really make sense to you. Look for patterns and recurring dreams and don't ignore them. It's a signal of some kind.

Over the next week or so, track your dreams and make some time to explore the themes and patterns about what your unconscious mind is telling you.

184
Less Hustle. More Flow and Ease

In spite of all the rhetoric about the need to work more and sleep less in order to truly succeed, if you're not operating from the right heart space and out of a great state, then all the hard work in the world won't get you anywhere. Maximum effort pushing a door that's designed to be pulled will only leave you exhausted and frustrated.

When you take care of your state first, it enables you to operate out of flow and ease rather than endless hustle. You find that the doors are open, and opportunities present themselves abundantly.

Success always comes out of who you are being rather than what you're doing. Being relaxed and confident always gives you access to your best stuff, whereas being needy and desperate drives the results you desire away.

In today's world, hustle, being driven and busyness are celebrated and promoted as essential to success. It's like, if you're not working like a madman then what are you doing with your life?

The idea that the harder you work the more you get is perhaps some of the most misleading advice ever given. What's worse is the long-term cost to your health, happiness and relationships when you don't know how to rest.

Less hustle, more flow and ease.

185
Stop and Breathe

Breathing is undoubtedly the most simple and important aspect of daily life, even though we do it at least 20,000 times a day!

One of the simplest, most effective ways of improving your physical, mental and emotional health is to stop and breathe consciously. That is, become aware of your breath.

The air we breathe is the same air breathed by everyone who has lived and ever will live. We share the air with plants and animals. Trees recycle the carbon dioxide we breathe out and give us more fresh air to breathe in return. Dying stars have produced all the elements in air so we actually breathe in the universe.

We are said to be alive when we take our first breath, and we die after we take our last. We breathe life. Our breath will respond and adjust according to what you're thinking, feeling, observing or experiencing at the time. It is intimately connected to your physical, emotional and spiritual state. Take a moment to stop and breathe today. It will be the most important thing you do.

186
You are Stronger Than You Think

I talk to so many people who constantly believe they're weak, broken and incapable of greatness. That's why they settle for stuff they really hate and just survive in dysfunction. Yet there's no such thing as an unresourceful person, just an unresourceful state. This means you definitely already have all that you need to flourish.

So much of the way the world works is about keeping people afraid and small by swamping them with lies about how incapable they are. Then, these people will do what they're told and let the rich and powerful continue to make decisions on their behalf.

The truth is that you're stronger than you think — I promise. You're capable of some epic stuff on this earth. You were made for a purpose and it's time for you to stand up and find your voice. Yes, you'll experience failure, disappointment and rejection at times. Yes, the system will threaten to take away all the benefits it provides, but you'll be ok.

Stop worrying about what might go wrong and be excited about what could go right. You really are stronger than you think.

187
Multitasking Misconception

Did you know that multitasking is impossible? Our brains can actually only do one thing at a time. While it may appear possible to listen to music and study simultaneously, your brain is either 100% focused on one or the other task.

It's constantly switching. Every time it switches, it has to shut down the software program for one task and reload the software for the other task, which, as you can understand, is actually very inefficient. It's in the switching of tasks that we leak the most of our daily energy budget.

Research also shows that, in addition to slowing you down, multitasking lowers your IQ. It causes mistakes, stress, lower productivity and it even affects your memory.

In order to be at our best, we have to be entirely present. Each task requires a specific mindset, and once you get in a groove you should stay there and finish. It's far better to do similar tasks in batches before moving onto something different rather than chopping and changing.

The key is to be present. Be here. Do one thing at a time and do it well.

188
The Illusion of Safety

Helen Keller[47] was an American author, political activist and lecturer. Born in 1880, she was the first deaf and blind person to earn a Bachelor of Arts degree. Her teacher, Anne Sullivan, was an equally remarkable woman as she had to break through the isolation imposed by a near complete lack of language, allowing the girl to blossom as she learned to communicate.

My favourite quote from Helen is 'Life is either a daring adventure or nothing. Security does not exist in nature. Avoiding danger is no safer in the long run than exposure.'

It turns out that playing it safe in life is one of the least safe things we can do! Security is an illusion. You may be avoiding some dangers by hiding, but there are a whole bunch of other dangers that hiding is actually exposing you to that are slowly killing you.

Remember, no one is getting out alive. What a terrible waste of life it would be to hide yourself away for fear of what could go wrong, all while it's already going wrong.

189
You've Changed

Have you ever heard someone sling the 'you've changed' line at others as though they'd committed some kind of crime? What's really happening behind this comment is that someone else's growth is threatening their own lack of growth and making them feel insecure and inadequate. 'You've changed' is then used as an attack in order to undermine the threat and keep others the way they've always been.

Yet everything that is alive changes. Constantly. If you plant a tree in the garden, in five years you'd sure hope it had changed! So why is it when people devote themselves to learning and development, constantly exposing themselves to new ideas and better ways of doing work, life and relationships, that the change they experience is somehow seen as a bad thing by others?

'You've changed' is actually a wonderful compliment. If you're not growing as a person, you're dying.

It's an interesting choice to give up on yourself and stop growing, but please don't be critical of those who have valued themselves enough to change and keep changing.

190
Self-acceptance

Why is self-acceptance and self-love so hard? Why is self-judgement and internal criticism so easy and natural? Why are self-limiting beliefs more common than empowering ones?

The answer has to do with the fact that our self-protection instinct is hardwired into every cell in our body. We do whatever it takes to be safe. We believe subconsciously that we're safe in groups. We don't want to be cast out of the group, so we 'conform' to fit in with the rules and expectations of our tribe.

We downplay our value and worth so we don't stick out from the crowd or do anything that may be frowned upon. Yet our go-to strategies cause us to hide and live small lives. They leave us feeling insecure and needy when we don't get the affirmation and acceptance we feel we need from others.

The great news about insecurities is that they're works of fiction. Just because they're our default doesn't mean they're true. We fear we're not enough, but the moment we actually journey courageously to the origin of that story, it proves to be just that — story.

We have always been enough and always will be.

191
Be Anyone You Want

....

You can be anyone you want, as long as you're willing to let go of needing the approval of those who think they know you.

So often we get stuck in a certain way of being, simply because this is how the people in our world expect us to continue to be. But surely being human is about our ability to grow, change, develop, learn, adapt and reinvent ourselves as many times as we're able, to get the most out of life.

Don't be limited in your journey of self-discovery and self-expression by the insecurity of those around you. Be willing to let go of needing their approval or permission to be who you really desire to become.

The moment you attach your identity to one story, you lose and you'll be stuck there for life.

Find a story that works for you. The moment it stops working for you, let go of it and find a new story. Don't tie yourself to one way of being, one pattern of living, one way of defining yourself or one way of relating to others.

192
Submitting to a Teacher

One of the most difficult and important aspects of reaching your potential in life involves voluntarily submitting yourself to a series of teachers.

To admit you don't know everything and then to place yourself at the feet of a master requires great humility and the death of ego.

However hard it is, and whatever sacrifice is involved, there's no other way to achieve your own level of mastery without becoming a student of someone else's mastery first.

In the stories of the greatest masters, past and present, there are always seasons of trial and testing where all of their future powers were in development. A central aspect of these experiences is submitting themselves to the teaching of someone further down the path.

Bestselling author, Robert Greene, describes step two of the process of mastery as 'apprentice with intensity'.[48] To take on an apprenticeship with intensity means being all in. It's about welcoming challenges that will strip you back to nothing and then rebuild you into a person of substance.

There are no shortcuts to this process and there's no other way. Who are you submitting to right now?

193
Peak Performance

Great coaching can be summarised as helping people achieve two things. Firstly, it's to gain great clarity about exactly what they want and secondly, to know exactly who they need to be to achieve it.

Developing well-formed outcomes and the ability to access the relevant high-performance state to achieve these well-formed outcomes is the essence of peak performance in any domain.

The big mistake most people make, that locks them out of this space, is that when they get clear about what they want, they imagine the next step is simply to focus on what they need to do to achieve their goals.

Yet, exploring what you need to do is never the path towards true peak performance. In fact, pursuing this course of action is guaranteed to leave you far short of your desired outcome.

Instead, be very clear about what you want and then know for certain what kind of state you would need to be in to have access to this outcome.

Your biggest goals will always require you to become someone you've never been before in order to achieve what you've never experienced.

Being always precedes doing.

194
Letting Go

One of the most profound exercises in our personal development journey is the act of letting go. It's so counter-intuitive and counter-cultural, yet it's a central part of truly living well.

Some of the things I'm intentionally letting go of to make more room in my life for things of true value and worth are:

7. the need to define myself by what I do and to be constantly busy

8. the need to control my experience of life

9. the need to be liked, agreed with or approved of

10. the need to know everything that's going to happen

11. the need to be right

12. the need to get it right every time

13. the need to help every person I talk to

14. the need to stay in the safe, known and familiar

15. the need to compare myself with others.

It's like Tarzan swinging through the jungle. In order to grab the next vine, he has to be willing to let go of the one he's swinging on right now.

What are you willing to let go of that's no longer serving you so you're able to keep moving forward in life?

195
Illusions

A magician's greatest tricks always come as the result of clever misdirection. Having distracted the audience's attention away from the real action, the illusion appears real. In this way, a magician can completely bend our experience of reality.

The amazing thing is that we often use the same misdirection trick in our own life to alter our experience of reality. The problem is that the illusions make things worse, not better.

Here are some great examples:

1. The illusion of control — you control things outside of your control through anxiety.

2. The illusion of safety — hiding and playing small is somehow safer than backing yourself and following your dreams.

3. The illusion of comfort — self-medicating to escape our reality gives us real comfort.

4. The illusion of separation — you're somehow different and alone and independent from the life all around you.

5. The illusion of attachment — your value is somehow connected to what you do and what you own.

Turn the lights on or have a look behind the curtain at what's really going on, and you'll see a completely different reality!

196
The Right Framework

At school, copying your best friend's answers is called cheating. And at university, cutting and pasting from someone else's thesis is called plagiarism. Both of these things will get you in trouble, yet outside of these two contexts it turns out that mimicking others is actually a very important and necessary part of success in any area of life.

Neuro Linguistic Programming (NLP) is the science of modelling excellence because it turns out that success leaves clues. If one person can achieve something great, replicating their method and following their path exactly means others can achieve the same results.

When you find the people who've already got the results you want, examine exactly what they did that worked so well. If you deconstruct their method and follow the same framework, you can match their results for yourself. The truth is that there are already wonderfully successful frameworks for almost every area in which you'd like to improve your results.

There are frameworks for resolving conflict, creating great relationships, earning more money, losing weight, getting fitter, faster or stronger, making business work and learning languages.

All you really need is the proven framework and the willingness to follow it exactly until it gets you the results you're looking for.

197
How Does Change Happen?

New awareness, more choice and altered beliefs — you cannot NOT change when each of these three things are present in your life. When these three elements are part of your world, there's an inevitability to the process of lasting change.

1. New awareness

If you can't see it, how can you possibly change it? All change begins with seeing things with new eyes — a light bulb moment, a new perspective, a great question that unlocks a whole new level of learning or an understanding of why you're doing what you're doing.

2. More choice

More awareness always leads to more choice. We're all trying to bring peace and comfort to ourselves the best way we know how. If we had a better way, of course we'd use it. More choice flows out of the experience of gaining new and deeper awareness. It comes from realising that being stuck with limited choice is simply an illusion, and that we each have 100% choice about the things that matter most in our lives.

3. Altered beliefs

Behaviour is entirely a product of what we believe. Therefore, if your new awareness is leading to increased choice, and that alters what you believe is true, what is right or what is best, then your behaviour is automatically changed as well.

198
Resisting Change

When you think about making change in your life, it can often feel like part of you is resistant to the idea.

Here is a simple framework for having a conversation with that part of you to work out what the resistance is for.

1. Be honest about your current reality.

2. Be clear about how you'd like things to be instead, and why.

3. Be aware of any feelings of fear or uncertainty about your ability to make the change to get from where you are now to where you want to be.

4. Take a moment to notice exactly where in your body these feelings sit.

5. Imagine going inside your body and sitting next to the part that's resisting change.

6. Without judgement, ask that part 'What for?'

7. Learn as much as you can about the positive intention that part has in trying to hold you back from change.

8. Explore all alternatives that still meet this intention and also allow you to step forward into your desired outcomes.

9. Acknowledge yourself when you've agreed on a plan both parts of you are happy with that allows all resistance to dissolve.

199
What You Seek is Seeking You

Most people in life are seeking something more — a new job, a successful business, greater self-confidence, financial freedom, life balance or loving relationships.

The key is to find a place of peace and rest right now while you're also in the process of seeking what you want. This means maintaining gratitude for what is, while also desiring what is to come. It's to have peace and confident expectation at the same time.

Rumi, a 13th century Persian poet, said, 'What you seek is seeking you'.

If you understand that the object of your desire is also seeking you and that there's another realm at work bringing the outcome closer to you, it allows you to relax into a state of patience and calm rather than being desperate and needy.

Without finding this peace, the road toward that something new will be littered with obstacles, struggle and self-doubt. Find peace and the road will become smoother with delightful discoveries and growth opportunities along the way.

Be clear about exactly what you're seeking, and then know it's also seeking to be found by you.

200
Pretending not to Know

....

Almost every time you say you don't know what to do, you're lying to yourself. The challenge is not that you don't know what to do, it's that you don't want to do what you know.

The cost of knowing what to do is often very high. With this knowledge comes the responsibility of the appropriate action. As the old saying goes, ignorance is bliss. If you don't know, then you don't have to do anything.

The problem is that you do know. You're just pretending not to.

You do know what's right, you do know what you want, and you do know what's best for you. You're just pretending not to, so you don't have to do anything about it right now for the fear of facing the pain involved.

The thing is that although there's a cost involved in knowing, there's always a great cost involved in lying to yourself and suppressing the truth. The bliss of ignorance turns out to be a false economy and not owning what you know always leads to a very small life controlled by others.

What are you pretending not to know?

201
Finding Your Purpose in Life

Finding your purpose in life is hard work. The question of what you want to do when you grow up is difficult enough, let alone the deeper quest to find your true destiny.

Because these questions are so big and daunting, most people avoid them completely! So, here are a few simple steps to get you started down the path of connecting with true purpose.

1. Recognise that everyone has a unique purpose in life that can be known. It's just a matter of searching in the right places.

2. Say yes more often to what gives you life. One of my favourite mottos in life is to 'go where the life is'. Explore the things that resonate deeply with you. They're obviously connecting with something that's uniquely and inherently you.

3. Develop your strengths. The better you become at the things you're good at, the more you'll be able to contribute to the world in these areas. This contribution is likely to be linked to your purpose.

4. Be willing to fail as many times as it takes. It's highly unlikely you'll find your purpose at the first attempt. It may take a lifetime of searching, but it will always be worth it.

202
Keep Learning and Growing

What gets you started on the process of personal growth won't always be the same thing that keeps you growing. If you hang on to the first tool and make it everything, it can often become a place to hide behind and an excuse for you to stay in your dysfunction.

The 5 Love Languages,[49] by Gary Chapman, is a great example of this. The model presents such a useful framework to begin the journey of self-awareness. To understand your natural preferences for giving and receiving love within relationships is a very useful discovery, yet I'll guarantee that anyone with a great marriage has had to go way beyond the scope of this model to keep their relationship growing.

Having a label for what comes most naturally to you doesn't justify operating exclusively in that mode for the rest of your life. Just because you may be more comfortable showing love by what you do, doesn't mean you don't have to work out how to also develop your capacity to speak from your heart, be present, give thoughtful gifts and to be physically affectionate.

The inherent danger of a simple model is that it oversimplifies.

If the personal growth tools that got you started on the journey are now allowing you to hide or be self-righteous, it's time to move on again.

203
To Say Yes Also Means Saying No

If you say yes to everything, you're actually saying yes to nothing. Getting married is a great example of this principle. Wedding vows are about fully saying yes to one person, which means saying no to everyone else.

What's more, marriage isn't about a historical decision to say yes to someone, but a daily one. And unless you can say no to that person, then you can't say yes to them either. If you have to say yes out of obligation, or the fact that you're stuck together, then how is that a yes?

Yes and no must always go together.

What are you saying yes to at the moment? Are you really saying yes to it? Or are you operating out of a sense of duty or obligation because you can't really say no? It's the things you say no to that give true meaning to your 'yes'.

What things do you really want to say yes to? And for this to happen, what will you need to say no to?

204
Every Thought Strengthens or Weakens You

American psychiatrist and author, Dr Jeffrey Schwartz, says that you're not your brain.[50] Thoughts are merely suggestions. This means you don't have to indulge them no matter how loud and persistent these suggestions are! Every thought you entertain either strengthens or weakens you. Therefore, what you allow to happen in your mind has a massive impact on the quality of your life.

The thoughts you think are responsible for the chemicals your body releases into your blood stream. Happy thoughts release serotonin, whereas anxious thoughts release adrenaline and cortisol. Your mind and body are one system. What you do with one affects the other and vice versa.

When you allow a free-for-all upstairs and pay no attention to your thought life, you leave yourself vulnerable to being controlled by negative thinking that then flows into your whole body.

This is why integrating mindfulness and meditation practices into your daily rhythms are so essential to overall health and wellbeing.

205
Create a Life You Don't Need an Escape From

Addiction is all about escape. At a cellular level, we're all hardwired to avoid pain and pursue pleasure. The reason why substances and certain practices become addictive is because of the power they have to give us instant pain avoidance or instant pleasure.

All addiction is birthed out of the desire to escape the pain of our current situation and to deal with the discomfort of the real world. Everything we do is, in some way, an attempt to bring peace and comfort to ourselves.

Therefore, the more we take full responsibility for directing and shaping our own lives, the less we need to escape from the feeling of being a victim to a life created by someone else.

Embracing 100% choice also means you're aware you're choosing your experience in every moment. If you don't like your current experience, change it rather than seek to escape from it.

Drugs, food, pornography and work are the addictions of our day and age. Rather than fighting the addiction, address the reason the addiction is needed. The key is to create a life you don't need an escape from.

206
Self-sabotage

When trying to improve the quality of your life and achieve lasting change, it can often feel like you are your own worst enemy! Consciously, you may feel 100% committed to moving forward, yet subconsciously you're not ready for change and end up sabotaging your own success.

For example, you say you're committed to improving your health, yet you find yourself bingeing on junk food and avoiding exercise. You know that good sleep is very important for you to be at your best, yet you stay up late watching TV every night. You say you're ready for a relationship, but you keep yourself so busy there's never any time for meeting new people.

Because it's often highly illogical, most people deal with self-sabotage very ineffectively. Often the only strategy for change is to just try harder.

The only reason we sabotage our own success is that, subconsciously, we link more pain to achieving the outcome than the pleasure we will get. Self-sabotage is actually a self-protection strategy, and we only protect that which we value, so self-sabotage actually shows how deeply we love ourselves.

Understanding this, fighting against yourself to solve this problem is entirely futile.

207
Overcoming Self-Sabotage

There are three keys to dealing with self-sabotage more effectively than trying to fight against yourself to win. The only way forward is to lovingly negotiate an end to the war.

There is ALWAYS a reason you are self-sabotaging. Ask some decent questions of yourself and do some self-awareness work rather than just saying 'I don't know what's wrong with me'. Take the time to explore the intention behind your behaviour without judgement.

All actions from the subconscious are driven from the instinct of self-protection. We only protect that which we value, so the self-sabotage is actually coming from a place of deep love. Two great questions to get you started are: How is not achieving this goal serving me right now? and What is dangerous about getting the thing I want?

Have a conversation with yourself about the things that need to be addressed so your subconscious is happy to move forward and support your overall plans rather than resist them. The key to ALL lasting change is to work with yourself rather than to continue fighting against yourself. You need self-permission to succeed. Self-discipline only makes things worse!

208
Winning Lotto

While it's common to fantasise about winning lotto or having your life magically changed by some incredible event, gaining treasures you're not ready for inevitably leads to significant loss and unhappiness.

Marketing guru, Seth Godin,[51] says:

The reality is, you're going to have to fight for every single thing, forever and ever. It's really unlikely that they will pick you, anoint you or hand you the audience and support what you seek. No one will ever realise just how extraordinary you are, how generous, charismatic or caring.

He continues with:

That pretty much doesn't happen, except for just a handful of people who win some sort of cosmic lottery, who get 'discovered' at a drug store and made a movie star, who are on the fast track to CEO of the Fortune 500, who get the big label deal and the gold records, merely for being in the right place at the right time.

Those few people, it turns out, end up unhappy. You might imagine that you'd like to be in their shoes, but they spend every day feeling both entitled and fraudulent. You, on the other hand, get the privilege of the struggle, and of working your butt off to make a difference.

209
Relationship Rules

Here are some of my personal rules that have helped me in developing quality relationships:

1. Deal with all personal insecurity and neediness. Others only have the ability to hurt me when I need something from them. Insecurity is incredibly unattractive and undermines all relationships.

2. No obligation or expectation. There is nothing to prove and nothing to defend, so never do things that others want me to do just so they'll think well of me. I'm happy to do things I don't necessarily enjoy, but only because I've chosen to do them.

3. People are welcome to be in my world and become journeymen, yet I don't need them to be there. No one who treats me poorly survives. I take 100% responsibility to train people to treat me well.

4. Never sweep issues under the carpet. Never play games. Never do awkward relationships. Face the painful stuff and find a way through.

5. Always make time to invest in quality relationships. Love people sincerely and whole-heartedly. Be vulnerable and real with the people in my world.

210
Power and Grace

I have the word POWER tattooed on my left leg, and GRACE on my right leg. These two words represent the great paradox of life.

The word POWER is a reminder of how wonderous it is to be a human being. To be alive is to be powerful beyond measure. I have the capacity to create, solve, learn, grow, adapt, innovate and to bring things into being that have never existed before.

This word draws me into the truth that I've been given ridiculously potent gifts. The most incredible of these gifts being choice and responsibility. This means I'm exactly where I've chosen to be. My results are completely mine. I've constructed my entire experience of reality. No one is coming to save me. It is all me.

The word GRACE, however, is a reminder of how dependent I really am.

Even with all this power, I can't make the sun rise and fall each day. I have no ability to make it rain or cause grass to grow. I can't produce air. I am deeply dependant on the sun, moon, stars, trees, birds, bees and cows. I depend on life itself for every breath I take. In the grand scheme of things, I'm nothing and no one.

This word draws me into the truth that I am a part of the whole. I'm connected to everyone and everything. I'm alive only by the grace of God. This causes me to surrender. To trust. To be open. To ask. To be humble. To be deeply grateful. To take myself lightly. To remember that life is a gift and to cherish each moment.

211
Get a New Jumper

Underneath every issue in our lives is some kind of limiting belief about our own value and worth. The research suggests these beliefs almost always originate in our lives before we are seven years old. Almost every child lets go of their natural belief in their high level of inherent value because, as they grow up, their world doesn't always reflect that back to them, which hurts massively.

They make an incredibly loving decision to protect themselves from this pain. Instead of setting themselves up for a big fall each day by telling themselves how valuable they are, and then not getting that reflected back to them, they let go of their belief of being enough and making it other people's responsibility to make them feel valuable and worthwhile.

All self-protection comes out of self-love. This is their best chance of a winning strategy in life. If they didn't do this, many children wouldn't survive the emotional trauma of growing up in the real world.

The cool thing about limiting beliefs is that they are works of fiction. It's like a jumper that you've put on and never taken off. Every time you look in the mirror now, it's all you see, and every time you go out, it's all others see. The thing is that it's just a jumper. It's not who you really are. You've always been enough and always will be.

All self-protection comes out of self-love. And maybe it's time to get a new jumper!

212
Five Big Mistakes

Here are the five biggest mistakes people make when trying to improve their lives:

1. Behaviour management. Trying to change your behaviour, emotions or thinking without dealing with the underlying beliefs that have created these results in the first place.

2. Self-discipline. The strategy of trying harder, committing to more effort, energy and focus works really well — until you get tired. Willpower is a limited resource.

3. Still living out of an old story. Trying to improve the quality of your life without changing the story you're living out of can never work. The story you live out of dictates how life goes for you.

4. Self-judgement. Beating yourself up and applying the drill sergeant approach never works. Instead it just causes you to live out of fear and pretence.

5. Being unaware of the rewards of living in dysfunction. Until someone becomes aware of the payoff they get for living in a place they say they don't like, they'll ultimately keep gravitating back to it because it works for them.

When you're ready for real and lasting change, there's a clear process that's both simple and hard but works. I promise you it's the complete opposite of everything listed above.

213
Three Keys for Lasting Change

....

1. Realise you are not broken.
Behaviour, thoughts and emotions are simply the end of the assembly line coming from the factory of your beliefs. The results you're getting in every area of life are the EXACT results you have designed your system to produce. There's nothing wrong with you.

2. Realise you are not a victim.
While you may not have chosen what happens to you, you always get to choose your response. Therefore, you're exactly where you have chosen to be. Blame and excuse are fun and easy, but they give away all your power, leaving you entirely helpless. You can take the power back the moment you're willing to part with the payoff you got for giving it away in the first place.

3. Realise you are not your behaviour.
EVERY negative behaviour has a positive intention. We're very quick to label others and ourselves by what we do, yet all behaviour is an attempt to meet an underlying need. Only when you discover the intention of the behaviour can you hope to swap it with something better.

214
State is King – Part 2

There is no such thing as an unresourceful person, just an unresourceful state. This means if you can change your state, you're capable of some truly amazing stuff today.

You have everything you need inside you already. The only limitations exist in your heart and mind. The scariest thing about fully stepping into our magnificence is all the uncertainty it creates in our world. All kinds of new things open up. Some people respond well, and others are totally threatened by our success.

The key to stepping into success sustainably, therefore, is internal, resourceful certainty.

1. Back yourself
2. Believe in your ability to handle any situation
3. Take 100% responsibility for your results
4. Love yourself
5. Affirm yourself
6. Be kind to yourself
7. Dress well
8. Eat well
9. Walk tall
10. Don't apologise unnecessarily
11. Show up present and unguarded

Remember. State is king. If you can control your state, you can also control your results.

215
How is This Not a Problem?

One of my favourite coaching questions when helping people work through their issues is: How is this *not* a problem for you?

See, every single thing you tolerate or complain about, but don't change, MUST be working for you. On the surface it looks like you're losing, yet the reason you stay in that place is that underneath there's always a gain, reward or payoff.

A basic rule of human psychology is that in order to tolerate a primary loss there must be a secondary gain.

In all my years of coaching, I'm convinced this is the hardest and most confronting thing to see about yourself. This is because secondary gain ultimately protects you from the thing you're most afraid of about yourself.

You can resist the idea and swear it's not true all you like, but if it REALLY wasn't working for you, you would have changed it already.

Today, examine the things in your life that are not the way you'd like them to be. What benefits are you getting out of staying in this situation exactly the way it is? How is this not a problem for you?

216
The Parable of the Talents

One of my favourite Bible stories is the parable of the talents.[52] A rich landowner entrusts three servants to look after his affairs while he's away on business. Interestingly, he trusts different amounts of money to each of them.

To the first, he gave the equivalent of five years' wages. To the second, he gave three years' wages and the third servant received wages for one year.

On his return, he calls his servants together to give an account of what they did with the money. The first two had doubled what they'd been given, while the third buried his money for fear of losing it and still only had the original amount. The owner praised the servants who'd invested wisely but was furious at the servant who'd had no increase, telling him to leave immediately while giving his money to the guy who had the most.

I think there are two lessons here.

1. Comparison is always dangerous. In this world, some people get more than others. Who knows why, but they do. If you look at those with more, you feel cheated and unmotivated. If you look at those with less, you feel arrogant and unmotivated.

2. The basic expectation on each of us is simply to grow what you've been given. Whether it is much or little, your responsibility is to go and do the most with what you have.

217
Blame

When things are not going well in your life, blaming someone or something for your current results is so natural, easy and even enjoyable.

I mean, it just makes so much sense to be angry at injustice — all the unfair, unfortunate, wrong, bad, mean, sad and rude things that have happened to you. If only this hadn't happened. If only they hadn't done that. If only you hadn't been treated like that. If only …

The point is that you're totally within your rights to play the blame and excuse card again and again, because what happened to you is wrong and unfair, and it shouldn't have happened and you did deserve better.

The only problem with blame is it leaves you powerless to change anything. It gives you zero ability to improve your situation and instead you become a disempowered victim waiting on the world to change.

The only way to get better results in your life is to take responsibility for them.

Who or what are you blaming right now? What excuse cards are you playing? How's that working out for you?

218
Don't Attach Yourself to One Vehicle

Did you know that the thing you want is never about the thing, it's always about what the thing represents? You don't actually want more money — you want what you think more money will give you. This means it's dangerous to attach your happiness to getting the thing you think you want.

If it has to be a certain way, then what happens if that way becomes impossible or too costly? If you've attached your happiness to that thing, then you're in big trouble!

You see, the person with the most behavioural flexibility wins. Getting clear on not only what you want, but also why you really want it, will allow you to see beyond the vehicle to the true intention.

It's also essential to detach your identity and sense of personal significance from getting those things. If you can't work out how to be happy and significant here and now, then getting there won't change anything.

Instead of taking it as a personal hit when things don't work out how you anticipated, you are able to stay focused on your overall desire and redesign a new strategy to get you there.

219
Are You Ready for What You Want?

There's a very fascinating quote from Jesus that says:

You can't put new wine in old wineskins ... or else the new wine will break the old wineskin and be spilled. Put new wine into new wineskins, and both are preserved.[53]

A modern translation might be: careful what you wish for because you just might get it. If you get something you desire before you're ready for it, it can be a curse rather than a blessing. If you want something you've never experienced before, you must increase your capacity to handle it, otherwise when you do get it, it will ruin you and all gain will be lost.

A classic example of this is what happens when people win lotto. If you go from being poor to rich overnight without doing anything to change your capacity to handle wealth, it destroys you. Five years down the track, most new millionaires have less money, less friends and less happiness than before the win!

The key is to be very clear about the goals you have and, at the same time, keep growing, renewing and enlarging your capacity to handle bigger and better things so that when your desires are fulfilled, they don't ruin you.

220
Giving Advice

Giving advice to friends and family is always dangerous. This is primarily because the giving of advice is almost entirely about making the giver feel better and almost always makes the receiver feel worse.

How could someone possibly know what is best for you? How could they know what you should or shouldn't do? People say, 'If I was you, I'd do this …' The problem is, they're not you!

Advice is a judgement. There are times where it's useful and valuable but I'm sure we totally overestimate how often those times actually present themselves.

Next time, before giving advice, just ask these two simple questions in your mind:

1. Did this person ask for my opinion or are they just sharing something from their journey?

2. If they did ask for an opinion, did they REALLY mean it?
As author of *The Coaching Habit,* Michael Bungay Stanier,[54] says:

If you could just stay curious a little longer and not be in such a hurry to move to advice and action, that would make so much of a difference to the quality of your conversations!

221
Failing at What You Don't Want

In his famous commencement speech at the Maharishi University of Management in 2014,[55] Jim Carrey told the graduates that his father could have been a great comedian, but because he didn't believe it was possible for him, he gave up on his dream and opted for a safe and responsible job as an accountant instead. However, when Jim was 12 years old, he vividly remembered the day his dad was made redundant from this so-called safe job and found himself unemployed.

Carrey says he learnt many great lessons from his father, but the most important one was gained by watching his father's choices. Seeing his dad lose his job impacted him deeply. In that moment he realised you can fail at what you don't want, so you might as well take a chance on doing what you love.

It turns out that playing it safe ends up not being safe at all. In this lifetime you'll get hurt, you'll try and fail, you'll experience disappointment and trouble and pain. They're all guaranteed.

Knowing this, it kind of takes the pressure off! Like Jim says, you may as well have a go failing at the stuff that's in your heart to do and the things that give you life, rather than just failing at stuff everyone else says you have to do.

222
How to Give an Effective Apology

The idea that it just takes time to rebuild trust is naïve and simply untrue. When trust has been broken, what is actually required to rebuild it is, instead, an effective and thorough apology.

Here are four crucial steps to ensure you get back to ground zero in your relationship and are not stacking issues on top of issues.

1. Understand exactly WHAT you did wrong and how that made the other person feel. If you don't know what you did then you can't do the next step.

2. Understand and communicate WHY you behaved that way. If you don't know why you did it, how could you possibly prevent it happening again?

3. Apologise sincerely for HOW you made them feel. This is the place for empathy. Step into their shoes and see how it would feel to have been treated this way.

4. Put forward a believable plan about how and why things will be different in the future and how this is unlikely to happen again.

Conflict resolution may not be easy, but it's certainly not complicated. When issues are not resolved completely there's an inevitable build-up of resentment and guardedness, and erosion of trust. When these steps are followed, the walls come down, forgiveness can be given freely and trust rebuilt.

223
Choose the Path with the Best Story

So many people seem so paralysed by the need to make the right decision, they end up making no decision at all. In their mind they ask: What if I get it wrong? What if I make a mistake? What if I fail?

There are no right or wrong decisions — there are just decisions, followed by more decisions. Some of the best advice I've ever been given is this: when you're not sure what to do, pick the path that will give you the best story to tell.

When I was thinking about moving my family to Germany for nine months, I had no idea if it were right and if it would work. A key factor in pulling it all together and making it happen was thinking about the story I'd be telling about my life in 20 years' time. It seemed there were two clear story options:

1. There was this time we were thinking of moving to Germany to see if I could run my business from anywhere in the world, but there was too much uncertainty, so we decided against it.

2. We took a massive risk to step into the unknown and it was harder than I thought, but even the challenges and troubles meant we'd have a bunch of great stories!

When you're unsure what to do, choose the path that will give you the best story to tell.

224
The Opposite of Depression

....

Bestse ling author, Rob Bell,[56] says that despair is the mistaken notion that tomorrow will be exactly the same as today.

As soon as you can start to believe that creation is continually being unveiled and renewed in you, you'll discover that you're personally invited to participate in the ongoing creation of the world. This means that what you do matters, and that it's therefore impossible for two days to be the same, no matter how deep down a hole you may be.

Bell teaches that the opposite of depression is not happiness, it is curiosity from which flows all vitality. As you follow your curiosity, it's always the path to a bigger life and the way out of any small places you find yourself stuck in.

Treat yourself like a high school science experiment. Be totally curious about the affect small changes will make to your overall experience of life. If you can change one thing about this situation, maybe you could change absolutely everything about this situation!

225
No Guarantees

Humans cannot survive without certainty. We are creatures of habit and are wired for a sense of control and safety, yet often we look for certainty in all the wrong places. We want life to be full of ironclad guarantees so we can feel certain that life will pan out the way we desire. Therefore, we react very poorly when the opposite happens.

The only real certainty is that life is uncertain! I hate to break it to you, but there are no guarantees that things will work out for you. No one is promising:

1. if you love with all your heart, you won't get hurt

2. your creative ideas will work in the real world

3. you'll realise your potential in life

4. your risks will pay off

5. that every time you put your best stuff out there, people will love it

6. your first, second, third or even your 100th business idea will make any money.

Even knowing all of this, what else are you going to do? Honestly. Packing up and bunkering down is no more likely to give you the certainty you crave than taking your chances.

The game of life is high stakes! That's what makes it so wonderful and exciting. When you've rolled the dice at the roulette table of life 100 times and failed, roll it 101 times.

226
The Issue is Never the Issue

One of the things that quickly becomes apparent in almost every coaching session is that the issue is never the issue. Just because you think you've clearly understood what's going on in your life, doesn't mean to say you have.

Real problem solving always requires a high level of accuracy in discovering the true nature of the problem you're most looking to solve before you invest any time, money or energy into solving it.

While behaviour management is nearly always the default strategy for self-improvement, only a change in belief can produce a lasting difference.

Is the issue that you give too much of yourself to keep others happy, or that you believe there's nothing likeable about you without this behaviour?

Is it that you're afraid of public speaking, or that you're afraid you have nothing of value to contribute?

Is the issue with your weight that you're lazy and undisciplined, or that you believe people will reject you if you truly show up?

Knowing that the issue is never the issue is very useful. It reminds you about the importance of taking a moment to step back from your own self-assessment to make sure you've dug deep enough.

227
Ask *How* Can I, Not Just Can I

....

Anthony Robbins says that the quality of our lives is determined by the quality of the questions we ask ourselves.[57]

Here's an example of making a small adjustment to a simple question to drastically improve the quality and, therefore, the impact it has on your life. Instead of asking can I do this, ask yourself *how* can I do this?

By adding one word to the question it completely changes what happens inside your head when you hear it. The revised question causes your brain to assume that it can be done, allowing it to search for the way to make it happen. If it can't find a way, then a new way is created.

The power of a great question is that it changes what we're paying attention to. Of course, we're all incredibly creative and have the capacity for great problem solving, yet it's easy to live as though that were not true.

One simple way to access the best of yourself is by making sure you're asking the best possible questions. Try it out for yourself and see what happens.

228
Madness

Eckhart Tolle says that if you condensed the history of mankind down into the life of a single human being, that person would be undeniably labelled as a violent, psychopathic madman.[58] Madness is the correct word for the human condition. It's the only word that does justice to our predicament.

One of the most extraordinary things in the universe is our ability to survive in deep dysfunction. We may complain about and hate our terrible situation, but we'll still get up each new day and do it all over again.

Most people will go on surviving in dysfunction, right up to the point of madness. So many good people, despite their best efforts, go through life hurting themselves and others. It's the norm for most of humanity.

The good news is that there are ways out of the madness for those who are ready to find themselves and break free. The question is: Are you willing to face up to what lurks inside you?

229
Five Steps to Increasing Creativity

Whatever story you're telling yourself about your capacity for creativity, believe it or not we're all creative beings. This creativity can and should be cultivated. Here are five steps to increase your creativity, inspired by the work of Alan Iny.[59]

1. Doubt everything. Challenge your current perspectives. Contrary to popular opinion, doubt is a gift. All creativity comes out of doubting that what we currently see is all there is.

2. Explore options around you. There are always more options. Probe the possible. Our brain is still the most complex machine on the planet and is capable of more computations per second than any other thing.

3. Generate many new and exciting ideas, even if they seem absurd. Divergence is taking what already exists and exploring unimagined uses for it.

4. Converge. From the vast sea of possibilities, evaluate and select the best ideas that give you the best chance to produce breakthrough results.

5. Finally, re-evaluate relentlessly. No idea is good forever.

On top of this, studies show that linking certain things, such as a favourite space, a certain notepad, or a special hat, to being creative allows you to get into the zone for creativity far more quickly.

230
What to Do When Things are Hard – Part 1

Challenges, struggles and hard times are a natural part of life. This being the case, it's very important to know how to handle these hard times.

One of the first things to consider is to make sure you don't actually NEED things to be hard in order to feel good about yourself. Imagine if you were attracting, or even creating, extra challenges in your life just so you could fulfil your need to feel significant!

In order to sleep at night, we must square away with ourselves that we're decent human beings. One of the most common strategies to do this is to validate yourself by what you do. The more you do, the better you must be as a human.

It becomes common for people to demonstrate how awesome they are by how many hard things they can cope with at once. If you've got nothing to show for yourself, how can you prove your value?

Life is hard enough without inadvertently making it extra difficult. The last thing you need is to be creating and attracting more hard situations as your only means of self-validation.

Detach your identity from what you do. Cut off all external means of significance and replace them with internal ones. Take 100% ownership of your own value and worth. Your significance is not defined by what you do or have, or what others think of you.

231
What to Do When Things are Hard – Part 2

When you're facing real challenges in life, and things are hard, the key is to embrace the struggle without letting it sink you. The only way out is through.

Every time you run and hide, you undermine your self-esteem. Avoiding hard things only teaches you that you don't have what it takes to deal with life and that you need to keep running. This eventually erodes all self-confidence and leads you to believe you're not enough.

It's crucial to frame your expectations so that 'hard' is necessary and ok. The aim of the game is not to get to a place where there are no problems, but to be the kind of person who can overcome your current problems so that you face higher quality ones.

In some seasons, 'hard' is exactly what you need. It's the place of character building, soul searching and foundation strengthening. Everyone can do easy. It's what happens in the hard times that separate those who will thrive in life from those who'll end up just surviving.

232
Dealing with Self-doubt

Self-doubt can be one of the most powerful and painful obstacles to success. Yet, it is surprising and refreshing to discover that having a measure of self-doubt is also a natural and healthy part of succeeding in life.

The only people who have no self-doubt are those who have already given up on themselves and life. These people have opted for the relative safety of bunkering down into their comfort zone and refusing to venture into anything new, different or risky.

If you're experiencing any self-doubt, it proves you're having a go and that you're pushing the edges of what is safe, known and comfortable. If you want zero self-doubt, go sit on the couch and do nothing with your life.

Have a conversation with your self-doubt — without judgement. Listen to your fears and understand your concerns. Heed the warnings and wisdom from your subconscious.

Self-doubt can be your voice of reason, making sure you've thought through your game plan thoroughly. It's fine to negotiate with self-doubt once you've listened. It doesn't have to stop you.

233
How Well Do You Apologise?

....

Do you know people who are terrible at saying sorry?

As you've probably heard me say a number of times by now, behaviour is at the end of the assembly line. It's simply the by-product of our beliefs. So, what must a person believe about themselves to behave this way?

The underlying fear is that if they've been found out as doing something bad or wrong then that somehow means they're a bad person. They believe being proven to be wrong says something about them as a person. Saying sorry would be admitting that they're no good. The whole thing becomes incredibly personal and the cost of being wrong is too high.

A person who struggles to say sorry will never be able to change that behaviour until they face up to the underlying belief or fear that they're not enough.

On the other hand, the person who is quickly able to own their mistakes, back down and offer a heartfelt apology knows they're not their behaviour. They haven't tied their identity to being right and, therefore, saying sorry at appropriate times is natural and easy.

234
The Dragon in the Cave

Underneath every relational, emotional and even financial issue in our lives is some kind of limiting belief about our own value and worth. Dealing with these limiting beliefs is the most significant and important work we'll ever do. However, most people never face these fears because it feels so daunting.

Often the things we're most afraid of exist only as a reality in our mind. What's worse is that they go unexamined. This enables them to turn into fire-breathing dragons, ready to consume us at any moment.

When a person finally gets the courage to confront the fear, they discover that what looks and sounds like a fire-breathing dragon is merely a couple of mice playing silly buggers, projecting shadows with a candle and making an awful noise with a couple of tin cans.

The amazing thing is that overcoming your fear of not being enough is not actually about conquering the dragon. It's realising the dragon has only ever existed in your mind! There's no dragon. It was a work of fiction. You've always been enough and you always will be.

235
Removing Other Options

Anthony Robbins defines making a decision as the cutting off of all other options.[60] To say yes to something means you're also saying no to a bunch of other things.

Often people think that leaving their options open is a good thing, yet this can just leave you sitting in front of a whole bunch of open doors, too frightened to step through any of them.

When you're facing a key decision in life, by all means bring your best to the game to choose what is right for you, but the decision is not made until you've cut off the alternatives. In order to fully say yes to what comes next means eliminating all other options. Now you're really committed.

We crave certainty in an incredibly uncertain world. Ultimately, the only way to find real certainty is to embrace uncertainty and back yourself. Continuing to affirm that you're a clever, creative and resourceful individual who has all they need to succeed already is a crucial part of building this internal sense of certainty. Self-doubt has far less room to crowd your mind when you're operating from a place of internal certainty.

236
Get Over Yourself

Some of the toughest, yet best, advice you'll ever receive is to get over yourself.

To make life really work, it's essential that you come to the place where you stop taking yourself so seriously. No matter how significant you are, it's highly unlikely the future of the planet is dependent on you. Yes, you're special and unique but the world will keep turning without you. It's not all about you.

Never before, in the history of the world, have we been so encouraged by society to think we're awesome, special and capable of doing anything we put our minds to. This is great, but at the same time it can make us feel too precious about our life and leave us feeling we're at the centre of the universe.

To get over yourself is not to feel that you don't matter, it's just to settle down a bit and be real about taking your place as part of a global community. This relaxed approach allows you to give yourself more room for playfulness, curiosity and adventure. If you're always under massive pressure to get everything right all the time, doubt and fear will cripple you.

237
Measuring Success

My favourite morning ritual at the moment is having three soft-boiled eggs on thick vegemite toast with avocado and spinach. It gets washed down with ice-cold OJ and I finish off with a cup of coffee. I like to scroll through the morning news at the same time, while trying to avoid getting egg yolk all over my phone.

One morning, while enjoying this delicious breakfast, I was reflecting on how best to measure success. I came up with a few questions.

In this moment:

1. am I lacking anything?

2. is there anything missing from this experience?

3. is there any place I'd rather be?

4. is there anything I'd rather be doing?

If the answer is 'NOPE!' then I'm totally succeeding at life. Sometimes I still fall into the trap of focusing on what I don't have and what I haven't done. This makes me feel like I'm somehow failing.

The truth is that all we have is this very moment. Yesterday has gone and tomorrow hasn't arrived yet. Be here — now. If your experience of now isn't the way you'd like it, then change it.

If it's the way you'd like it to be, then you're being entirely successful.

238
When You're Not Sure What to Do

When you don't know what to do, or you feel stuck or lost in life, the best plan is to return to your key decision-making frameworks. What are your foundational principles of happiness and success? What are your key values and non-negotiables? When everything else is uncertain, this is the bedrock from which you build a life of substance.

Having key decisions that you've already made means that when everything seems up in the air and uncertain, there are key guidelines in place to stop you having to go all the way back to the start and reinvent your life.

When you're in a place of doubt, work from the known to the unknown. Come back to the things that you know are true (to the best of your understanding) and then move into solving questions about the things you don't know.

When self-doubt takes over, it can feel like everything is uncertain in your life. Yet, this is actually never true. Reminding yourself of what you do know helps you be more relaxed about what you don't know.

If you're not clear on your own set of guiding principles, this could be the most important place to start.

239
You Need a Lot Less Than You Think You Do

One of the most profound and life-changing experiences I've had was while rock climbing on the east coast of Tasmania.

As a complete novice rock climber, my coach somehow convinced me to abseil down a 60-metre beach cliff, only to inform me at the bottom that the only two options to get home were to climb out or swim out!

The rock face in front of me looked like a sheet of glass and I was convinced that the task ahead of me was entirely impossible. Yet somehow I made it to the top in one piece. It turns out I needed a lot less grip, skill, strength and strategy than I thought I did.

Off the back of that key learning, moving my family to Germany for nine months was exactly the same thing. In order to survive, we needed so much less certainty, strategy and financial security than we (and others) imagined we would.

Life is like that. It's impossible to be fully prepared for any situation. Sometimes you've just got to say yes and work out the rest later. I'm not encouraging recklessness, but most people really err on the side of caution and in doing so, let life pass them by.

It's highly likely that you need a lot less than you think.

240
Adding to the Noise

There are three key parts of the human brain.

1. The reptile brain — in charge of flight or fight instinctive responses.

2. The mammal brain — in charge of motivation through pleasure and pain, and reward and punishment.

3. The human brain — the rational, cognitive decision maker.

4. Interestingly, all information has to go through the reptile brain first. This means everything is filtered for safety before being passed along the line to eventually be processed rationally. The key question processed here is: Is this a threat to my time, energy, money, beliefs or physical safety?

If someone is speaking to you and it's boring, irrelevant, incoherent or silly, your brain actually blocks it straight away. It's deemed a dangerous waste of your time and energy, which means you're actually not listening and are instead focusing on the quickest way out of the conversation.

It's a privilege to be heard by others — don't take it for granted. If you want your message to be received and processed thoroughly, you have to pitch things more carefully. The reptile part of the brain is just like the lyrics of one of Switchfoot's songs: 'If we are adding to the noise please turn off this song!'[61]

If you're just adding to the noise, you'll be blocked every time.

241
Don't Lose Sight of What You Want – Part 1

I'm always banging on about the importance of being very clear about what you want in life. Having a clear and compelling picture of how you'd like your life to be is the ultimate leverage for change.

On the other hand, here are eight painful things that happen when you lose sight of what you really want.

1. You end up serving other people's agendas for your life.

2. By ignoring and suppressing deep desire, you diminish your humanity.

3. You settle and survive, and life becomes something to endure.

4. You lower your expectations of what is possible.

5. When you lower expectations, you may avoid disappointment in your life, but you also eliminate joy.

6. You use ugly terms like 'it is what it is' and 'you've gotta do what you've gotta do'.

7. You have to work hard at convincing yourself you're happy.

8. You become an entitled consumer and get very upset when others make decisions that threaten your privileges and comforts.

Perhaps it's time to take control of your life and refocus on what you really want in life, rather than settling for what you don't want.

242

Don't Lose Sight of What You Want – Part 2

....

Here are 12 more painful things that happen when you stop being clear about what you want in life.

1. You end up making all decisions based on the fear of what you could lose and what could go wrong.
2. You become boring.
3. You stop adding something unique and valuable to the world.
4. One day rolls into the next. Life loses its colour and taste.
5. Blame and excuse are your constant companions.
6. You forget what you're really capable of.
7. Anything that threatens your comfort zone creates significant anxiety.
8. You convince yourself you're a victim of your circumstances.
9. You constantly compare yourself to others who seem to have been given a better or easier life than you: 'If only I had what they have, life would be so different'.
10. You develop a range of bad habits and self-medication strategies that give you a temporary escape from the crap life you've created for yourself.
11. Time goes incredibly fast and slow simultaneously. Each day drags on. You're always looking at the clock, but each year is the same as the last one. Life becomes a blur.
12. You fantasise about winning lotto or getting lucky on the pokies as the solution to all your problems.

Maybe it's time to take control of your life and refocus on what you really want in life rather than settling for what you don't want?

243
Insecurity Will Cost You

Insecurity is the cause of all madness in life. It causes inherently good people to consistently hurt themselves and others.

There are four areas where insecurity costs you the most.

1. Relationships. Insecurity in relationships causes you to be needy. You crave love and attention, but when you get it, you doubt it. Two insecure people in a relationship drain each other until there's nothing left.

2. Finances. Insecurity causes you to doubt your value as a person, meaning you consistently settle for less than you're worth. It also means you never feel you deserve any better.

3. Work. Insecurity keeps you on the back foot, causing you to miss opportunities and doubt your ability. It makes you suspicious of others and you take everything personally. You get walked all over and taken for granted.

4. Health. Patterns of sickness, extra weight and even skin issues, all flow out of limiting beliefs about yourself.

Insecurity, left untreated, will eventually destroy you. The good news is that all insecurity is based on a lie and there is a clear way to live totally secure in who you are.

244
The Best of You Behaving Badly

It's impossible to do self-judgement and self-awareness at the same time. When you take judgement out of the equation you're then able to see what's going on and why it's happening.

One of my favourite questions about behaviour comes from my long-time mentor, Greg Bellingham:[62] What if this is the best of you behaving badly?

Rather than judging your anger, frustration or annoyance as bad, what if it was your most honest, creative, authentic self, rising up and acting out? It doesn't justify the behaviour, but if you can understand it, it allows you to honour the best of you and channel it in a more resourceful way.

It's like a creative kid who gets labelled as naughty because there's no outlet for his talent in the confines of the classroom. His behaviour may actually come from his desire to contribute meaningfully.

Change only comes through genuine awareness and understanding. For this to happen, it's crucial to let go of the self-judgement and realise you're not your behaviour.

245
Judging Others

Judging others is actually an attempt to make yourself feel better. Contrary to what you might think, it has nothing to do with improving the life of the person you're being critical of.

One of the least resourceful ways of meeting your need for significance as a person is comparison. If you can point out other people's weaknesses and poor decisions, it helps you prove that you're better than them, which then helps you feel better about your own life.

This can manifest as bullying, road rage, gossip, slander, cruel jokes and worse. It's such an ugly and unattractive strategy! Sure, we all need to feel good about ourselves, but if you need to resort to judging others to do so, it might be time to go into a room full of mirrors and have a good hard look at yourself.

Is that really who you want to be? Is that how you want others to treat you? Is there a more resourceful way to feel good about your life than trampling on others to elevate your status?

Ultimately judging others will never make you feel good about yourself long term and will always cause pain for others too.

246
Time – Money – Mobility

In his outstanding book, *The 4-hour Work Week*,[63] Tim Ferriss suggests that the three real luxuries in life are time, money and mobility.

The interesting thing is that most entrepreneurs have none of the three. Even if what they're doing is seen as successful, it often takes up all their time, their money is invested into their business and they're stuck in a specific location.

The key, therefore, is to create products and services that can operate without you being in the room and that you can manage remotely. With technology the way it is these days, this literally means you could be anywhere in the world and have clients anywhere in the world.

The amazing thing about the world we live in is that there has never been an easier time to make it as an entrepreneur. There really is no barrier to entry. You don't have to ask anyone else's permission, and no one can really stop you.

As you grow and develop yourself as a person, it's all about bringing what's uniquely inside you to the world with the courage and skill to provide solutions people are willing to pay for.

Time, money and mobility can become a definite reality if you're prepared to leave the relative safety of the 9-to-5.

247
Jump Off the Merry-Go-Round

Sometimes the only way to stop being affected by other people's silly games is to get off the merry-go-round altogether. After all, you can't lose a game that you're not even playing!

One of the most important discoveries, in terms of your own mental and emotional health and wellbeing, is to realise that not all difficult relationships have to be restored and not all people will be able to be true companions in your life.

Sometimes people lose the ability to flow together for whatever reason. Fighting for a relationship that has come to the end of its season can be incredibly taxing and unfruitful. It's impossible to keep everyone happy all the time.

It's crucial to assess the direction of your life and the things that are most important to you, rather than continuing to do laps of the merry-go-round in relationships that have become dysfunctional and even toxic.

Rather than trying to win the relational games that are being played, sometimes the only way forward is to stop playing the game all together.

248
Who Do You Say You Are?

I'm constantly astounded by how much power we have as human beings. When you stop and look at what we're capable of, it's absolutely stupendous. Yet, most people live safe and small lives without any real power to affect the results or direction of their life.

People most commonly feel that the quality of their life is determined by what others say about them. They constantly crave attention and affirmation from friends, family, colleagues and even God. When people say good things about them, they feel enlarged and strengthened. But when others are critical or negative towards them, they end up deflated and discouraged.

One of the most amazing things about life, however, is our own opinion of ourselves is the only one that really counts. Ultimately, it all comes down to who you say you are.

We are sense-making creatures who constantly have to decide what things mean. We filter every experience and conversation through our own beliefs to find evidence for whatever we believe is true. If you believe you're no good, it doesn't matter what anyone else says, you'll continue to find evidence to support this belief.

Who do you say you are? This is the most important question.

249
Twelve Signs of Insecurity

I get that no one wants to be called insecure. But in a judgement free space, here are a few key indicators that you have some insecurity to deal with in your life:

1. Everything feels personal.
2. You're overweight and unhealthy.
3. There's arrogance, pride, ego, selfishness or even narcissism.
4. You're always defensive.
5. You can't apologise and have no reverse gear.
6. Jealousy eats at you.
7. You put others down with gossip and slander.
8. You find energy in holding a grudge towards certain people.
9. You often overreact and are excessively emotional.
10 Blame and excuse are constant companions.
11. You are angry and frustrated at others all the time.
12 You have to have the last word.
13 There's always something to prove and defend.

Don't worry — this doesn't make you a bad person. But, if you don't deal with the insecurity in your life, it will destroy you. My most favourite thing in the whole world is showing people how to live free from all insecurity.

250
Limiting Beliefs Have a Payoff

Ultimately, all my coaching work comes back to helping people deal with self-limiting beliefs about themselves. The first part of the operation is helping people to see what they really believe. The second part is about helping people let go of the belief which has, in many ways, become their friend over the years.

The interesting discovery is that all limiting beliefs actually serve us on some level. In fact, they keep us safe from facing the things we're most afraid of.

For example, if you have a belief that sharks are waiting to eat you the moment you dip a toe into the ocean, then this belief actually protects you from that fear being realised, because it's incredibly unlikely that you'll ever go swimming at the beach.

The same is true with beliefs about yourself. If you fear you're not enough, this limiting belief will keep you from ever putting yourself out there in situations where you could be found lacking.

In order to be free from this belief, you need to be willing to let go of the protection it provides through developing a clear focus on what you really want for your life instead.

251
Complaining is Madness

When you are down on your luck and things are not going well, it's easy to fall into the trap of complaining about your life and how hard it is to be you.

WNow while complaining about a situation that isn't ideal is very natural and common, it actually doesn't make any sense.

Eckhart Tolle says that when we complain, we become disempowered as we make ourselves victims. His advice, therefore, is to leave the situation, change the situation or accept it. All else is madness.[64]

Complaining will cause you to live with the illusion of no choice and give away your power for change. It is to pretend that you are not in charge of your responses and that you're not exactly where you've chosen to be. It always leaves you feeling hopeless and helpless.

People who find a way to win in life never complain. They understand that no matter how bad things are, or how much pity they may crave, complaining makes no sense at all. All it does is make things worse and keep them in a place they don't want to be.

The wisdom from the stoic philosopher, Marcus Aurelius, is this: Don't be overheard complaining. Not even to yourself.

252
What are You Keeping Track Of?

When interviewed by Tim Ferriss on his podcast, Seth Godin said most people get stuck in a cycle of keeping track of the wrong things.[65] They're constantly thinking about how many times they've failed, been rejected or had things not work out the way they wanted.

Keeping track of those things will only cause you to end up feeling frustrated and discouraged. Why not keep track of other things — like all the times things did work out instead? Track all the risks that paid off, all the great things people say about you, the things you're good at and all the times you were able to brighten someone else's day.

Godin says that when we start doing this, we're able to redefine ourselves as people who make an impact on the world. Whatever you pay attention to, you get more of. Whatever you measure begins to define you. When you track and measure the wrong things, these wrong things just keep showing up in your world.

What are you measuring and keeping track of? Are you paying more attention to your wins or your failures?

253
Courage Over Confidence

When it comes to real world results, courage is definitely more important than confidence.

People often wait until they feel more confident before doing the things that they've always wanted to do, but that's actually not the path to success. If you're waiting for confidence to show up in the mail, you'll be at the mailbox for the rest of your life.

Courage is far more important than confidence anyway. And often, all it takes is 30 seconds of courage for you to step up and grab key opportunities with both hands. Even just pretending to be confident for a mere 30 seconds could be all that's between you and your next big breakthrough, opportunity, relationship, job, business or friendship.

Interestingly, there are very few noticeable differences between real confidence and people pretending to be confident. Often, the people who appear most confident in life are simply those who are prepared to put their pride on the line and have a crack in a moment of sheer courage.

Confident or not, what do you want and what are you prepared to do about it?

254
Uncomfortable Conversations

Tim Ferriss says that one of the key indicators of a person's success in life can usually be measured by the number of uncomfortable conversations he or she is willing to have.[66]

It seems there are two types of people in life — peacekeepers and peacemakers. For the sake of keeping the peace, the first type of person avoids the uncomfortable conversation and therefore, never speaks to the elephant in the room.

While the immediate benefit of this strategy is surface-level peace, the peacekeeper suffers with the anxiety of unresolved situations and the pretence that things are better than they really are. While you go on tolerating the things in your relationships that aren't right, you must suffer in silence. These things end up eating you from the inside out and undermining your self-esteem.

To be a peacemaker, on the other hand, requires the courage to have the uncomfortable conversations when they're painfully necessary. Rather than playing games or pretending everything is fine, they lean into conflict so that things can be resolved.

The immediate cost is obviously the discomfort of addressing the tough stuff, but the long-term reward is deep relationships and internal peace.

What uncomfortable conversations are waiting to be had in your world right now?

255
Rest

In a world where busyness is the most socially accepted addiction of our day, rest is almost a dirty word. However, if you desire to flourish in life, rest is one of the most important elements to master.

Learning to find a rhythm of rest that allows you to be at your best when it matters most AND being able to totally switch off in order to rest and recover without feeling guilty, is some of your most crucial work in life.

Here are five ideas to get you started:

1. Discover the power of managing your energy instead of your time. Energy really is your most valuable resource and state is king.

2. Break the connection between your work and your value. You are not what you do. You have the exact same inherent value when you're doing plenty and when you're doing nothing.

3. Cut off the need for approval and acceptance from others. You'll need reference points for internal success and significance in order to rest without guilt. No one else will give you permission to rest — that's your job.

4. Plan adventure, fun, rest and recovery into your calendar. If you try to squeeze rest into leftover time, it always gets eaten up by other things first.

5. Begin with the end in mind. Be clear about how you'd like your life to be five years from now and set a clear intention. Move things into place from today so this becomes your reality.

256
Don't Make Decisions Out of Fear

When my wife and I clocked up 20 years of marriage it meant we'd been together for more than half our lives. Obviously, we made commitments to love and honour each other, but one other promise we made in our first year of marriage that has served us incredibly well, was never to make decisions for our future based on fear.

Whenever it seemed like we were under pressure or at risk of something bad happening, we would instead focus on the kind of people we wanted to be and the kind of life we wanted for our family. Then we operated out of that space.

As Nelson Mandela said: 'Let your choices reflect your hopes and not your fears'.

Every time you make choices out of fear, you move towards a smaller place and you shrink the scope of your life. And every time you allow your hopes to guide your decisions, you end up becoming enlarged and your heart leads you to a much more abundant space.

Next time you're faced with a big decision, or even small daily decisions, notice whether it's your hopes or your fears that are guiding your decision-making.

257
It Is What It Is

....

'It is what it is' has to be one of the strangest phrases in common language today. The moment it's used to describe your situation you're powerless to alter anything about your experience. What if it's not what it is?

Five people who are all observing the exact same event will all have different experiences and will therefore tell different stories about exactly what happened and why.

If it is what it is, then we're merely victims of our environment. We're passive bystanders who are affected by the life that's happening all around us but powerless to change it.

What if we actually have the power to cause the results in our life rather than passively living in the effect of what others are causing for us? What if we move from being a passenger on the bus to becoming the driver?

People who do life well are always aware of the abundance of choice they have to shape their own experience. They look at the world in a way that fills them full of hope and faith and love. They let every experience add to the quality of their life and give them more of what they want.

It is whatever you make of it.

258
Optimising Happiness

It's possible to optimise all kinds of things in life, so why not optimise your happiness as well? Rather than just going with the flow all the time in terms of what's supposed to make you happy, we each have the chance to optimise our own happiness by exploring the things that truly do make us happy.

For instance, others might suggest an expensive new car will make you happy, but you might discover a brand new car makes you only 10% happier for only three months, whereas a cheaper second-hand car and two international holidays would be the same price, but make you far happier for longer.

You might be 10% happier for one month after getting a pay rise and promotion at work yet moving out of the city and earning less money may in fact make you 80% happier for five years.

The point is, give yourself permission to find what works best for you and to go where the most life is. Doing life well is all about taking responsibility for your own happiness rather than letting others dictate what you must do in order to be happy. Optimising happiness is a great part of getting to know yourself and designing a life you don't need an escape from.

259
Keep Growing

It's not uncommon for people stuck in 9-to-5 jobs to develop a sense of entitlement that they strongly deserve job security with guaranteed benefits and rewards. While workplace agreements are important, looking for eternal safety from your boss is problematic and misguided.

What these people often fail to remember is that they are benefiting from the courage and risk of their employer whose entrepreneurial spirit created the job in the first place.

While it may have been a massive stretch and represented real growth for you to land the job in the first place, if you're still in the same role five or 10 years later, chances are it's now killing you.

The point is that pain is a gift designed to bring a loving message. Pain tells you something needs changing. It tells you that you were meant for more, that your talents are being wasted and that there's more inside you desperate to come out. The pain of your job may be telling you it's time to spread your wings and fly again.

Keep growing. Keep exploring the limits of what you're capable of. Keep following the desires of your heart. Grow or die.

260
My Top Three Personal Development Tips

I'm often asked for the quickest way to change your life or for shortcuts to get more of what you want. While oversimplifying things is always dangerous and magic pills never work, if I had to pick the three most important keys to lasting personal improvement, here are the ones I'd choose:

1. You've got to know exactly what you want and who you need to be to get it. Set very well-formed outcomes and then embody the kind of person who has access to those results.

2. You've got to let go of self-judgement. There's no right or wrong, good or bad. There's only stuff that works and stuff that doesn't. Letting go of self-judgement allows you to adapt, change and correct your course quickly and without fuss. You can't do self-awareness and self-judgement at the same time. This allows you to separate behaviour from intention, which is absolutely essential in the process of lasting change.

3. You've got to accept that all we have is story. Reality is just your perception — you can change it if you want to. You're not the actor in the story, you're the storyteller. People who succeed in life always tell better stories than those who struggle.

261
The Power of Being Relaxed

The human body can produce amazing results under stress, yet we're actually at our most powerful and creative when we're calm and present.

As we relax, the frequencies of our brain waves become slower and deeper and we gain access to our most dynamic internal resources. Memory, creativity, problem-solving and intuition are all best accessed from this low-frequency state of being.

The moment our blood pressure rises, and we perceive we're under threat, our body diverts all energy and attention to self-defence, protection and survival strategies. There's no remaining budget allocation for the energy that needs to be sent towards growth and development instead.

The best sports stars, leaders and businesspeople are at the top of their field due to their capacity to be relaxed, even when under great pressure. They keep their cool and therefore always have access to their best stuff when they need it most. More than that, they realise that sustained stress is one of the most toxic and dangerous things for our body to endure.

Therefore, activities that move us back towards a state of rest are ultimately an essential part of peak performance. Cultivating mindfulness, meditation and relaxation techniques into daily life may feel unproductive in the moment, but always pay great dividends in the long run.

262
Love and Fear

Named by *Time Magazine* as one of the 100 most important thinkers of the 20th century, psychiatrist, Elisabeth Kübler-Ross, says there are only two emotions — love and fear.[67]

All positive emotions come from love, while all negative emotions are, in some way, a form of fear. That is, love and fear are the two ends of the emotional spectrum and all emotions fit in between as part of these two.

This certainly simplifies things greatly when we examine the most common emotional responses. For example, we become angry when we fear being misunderstood or taken advantage of. Anxiety is the fear of our weaknesses or inadequacies being exposed. Frustration is the fear of not getting what you want.

On the other hand, excitement is the anticipation of experiencing what we love. Peace comes from the safety of being loved and joy is an abundance of love that overflows.

This means, in any moment you're able to stop and observe your own emotions and ask yourself if you're operating out of love or fear. The way out of fear is always into love and every time we move way from love it's into fear.

263
Living Between On and Off

Elite fitness instructor, Pavel Tsatsouline, says that today, most people live between the on and off switch.[68] His observation is that due to the increasingly busy and driven lifestyles that are common in western culture, people end up living with no ability to truly switch off and rest and therefore no ability to be fully on and engaged.

People feel guilty for resting and empty when they have nothing to do. Busyness is a status symbol, so people fill their lives with more and more roles and tasks. They understand that it's killing them, yet they seem to have no ability to get off the treadmill of life.

If you feel like you're constantly 'on', always moving from one task to the next without proper down time, then, in fact, you're never on. Instead, you're living in some half state of existence and performance.

Rest and recovery are completely essential in order to be at your absolute best when it matters most and to achieve peak performance. You have a limited amount of energy and if you spread it too thin, everything suffers. Being able to fully switch off is crucial to maximising energy levels for the most important roles and relationships.

If you never turn your battery off or fully recharge it, it's highly likely that you'll be operating on power-saving mode instead.

264
Raising Confident Children

I'm sure every parent wants to do as well as possible preparing their children for life. It's natural to want your kids to feel secure and confident, yet many parents struggle with knowing how to help their children develop these empowering beliefs.

If you're a parent, here are five ways to help your kids deal with insecurity and develop a healthy self-esteem.

1. Talk about it. More conversations are always better than less conversations. Because everyone is insecure about being insecure, no one talks about it.

2. Model what security and confidence look like. The biggest gift you could ever give your children is to show them it's possible rather than just telling them. Don't offer advice you're not using yourself.

3. Help them face up rather than run away. Every time they avoid hard things, they teach themselves they can't and that they're not enough, which undermines their self-esteem.

4. Show them their identity and value are separate from their behaviour. They're not 'good' if they do well and 'bad' if they do wrong.

5. Don't make them perform for your love. Love is the opposite of fear. There's no room for fear and insecurity when we feel totally loved for who we are.

265
A Believable Plan

One of the most common causes of internal conflict is not having a believable plan with yourself. You may have consciously decided to do something a certain way yet, subconsciously, there's no agreement or buy-in. This lack of cohesion inevitably leads to internal resistance and self-sabotage.

This may manifest as weight gain, injury, illness, anxiety, lack of energy, skin conditions or sleeplessness. There is internal conflict operating beneath the surface, robbing you of peace and causing you to feel unsettled.

The key to avoid these things in your life is to make sure you have internal agreement with your plans rather than just forging on, irrespective of the cost. Respect your own judgement. Honour what you know to be true, irrespective of what others want you to do.

Set up regular meetings with yourself to check in and make sure all is ok. While this may sound abstract and unusual, all flourishing in life comes through working with yourself rather than against yourself. Rapport with yourself is everything.

Where trust has been broken internally, the final part of restoring it is to develop a believable plan about how things will be different in the future.

266
Goal Setting

The harder you work on the setting of your goals, the easier they are to achieve.

Here are five keys to help get it right:

1. Do not proceed until you have a high desire for change. People often overestimate their readiness for change. Unless you have a compelling reason why things must be different for you, setting goals will probably be a real waste of time.

2. Speak to the fear. 'What do you want?' is the most dangerous and confronting question we could ask ourselves. Yet, even though it's a big scary question, it's ok because *not* asking it is twice as scary.

3. Always explore intention. No one actually wants the 'thing', they want what that 'thing' represents. Getting clear about the intention helps clarify what you really want so you don't get trapped into thinking it's about the vehicle getting you there.

4. Weigh all the consequences. Be careful what you wish for because you just might get it. Everything comes with a price. It makes sense to have done a cost analysis before you pull the trigger on your goals, otherwise achieving them may actually make you less happy.

5. Set clear measurements. If you can't measure it, you can't have it. Be as specific as possible in the setting of your goal and then determine very clear measurements to let you know when you're on track to achieve it.

267
Happiness is Found in Solving Problems

Bestselling author, Mark Manson,[69] says problems are a guaranteed constant in life. Problems never stop but merely get exchanged or upgraded. Happiness then comes from the solving of these problems.

If you're avoiding your problems, or feel like you don't have any problems, then you're going to make yourself miserable. The secret sauce of genuine happiness is in the solving of problems, not in the living with the absence of problems.

To be happy, we need something to solve. Happiness is therefore a form of action. It's an activity, not something that's passively bestowed upon you and not something you magically discover in perfect conditions.

It doesn't automatically appear when you finally make enough money to add on that extra room to the house or buy that new car. And you don't find it waiting for you in a place, an idea, a job or even a book.

Happiness is a constant work in progress because solving problems is a constant work in progress. The solutions to today's problems will lay the foundation for tomorrow's problems and so on. When you come to terms with this idea, it allows you to welcome new problems as an opportunity for more happiness.

268
Story – State – Strategy

The common path is to orient your life in this order: strategy, state, story.

Most people start the day by jumping straight into what needs to be done, despite being impacted by the state they find themselves in and with almost no awareness of the overarching story they're living out of. This is a recipe for a life of underachieving and frustration.

However, if you're looking for an unfair advantage in life, rearrange the order of these three words to: story, state, strategy.

This means, when starting your day, the first priority is an exercise of storytelling. Your work here is to identify and deconstruct any stories of lack or limitation and create and align yourself to empowering and beautiful stories.

Next, the key is to prime your state. Take 10 minutes to practise life-giving rituals that fill you full of energy.

Finally, you're ready to turn to action and strategy. From the position of being aligned to an empowering narrative and being in a peak state, you're now capable of doing your best work.

Remember: story, state, strategy. Not: strategy, state, story.

269
Honour the Gift

William Shakespeare lived and died in relative anonymity. In his own time, he was rated as merely one among many talented playwrights and poets, but since the late 17th century, he has been considered the supreme playwright and poet of the English language.

Shakespeare devoted himself to his art even though no one around him really paid much attention. He didn't receive the accolades, fame or fortune he desired until long after his death.

In fact, the same is true for many men and women we now celebrate and esteem, for their contributions that have changed the world, but who died without ever seeing the fruit of their labours or the fulfilment of their dreams. Even Jesus lived and died having only 10 to 12 close followers and a few hundred other supporters.

In spite of the challenges they faced and the lack of apparent success, each of these people honoured the gift inside them and did not sell out when things got hard.

What would it mean for you to honour the gift inside you in spite of whether or not you could see the impact of your work here and now?

270
Women and Personal Development

Men have all kinds of challenges that stop them doing personal development, but I wonder if a woman's greatest challenge, in general, is not to lose herself in the word 'mother'?

It's really common for mothers to position themselves as the suffering servant within the home and go last when it comes to having their needs taken care of. Investing in personal development kind of feels like they're being selfish by worrying about themselves first, instead of taking care of everyone else's needs as their role demands.

Here are three ideas to help you work through this thought.

1. Question your rules for how to be a good person. Are you only 'good' because you keep everyone else happy? Who taught you that? Is it true? Could there be a better rule?

2. Put your own oxygen mask on before helping others with theirs. The greatest gift you can give your kids is to model what it looks like to live life well. Don't just tell them — show them. You would need to believe that the most useful we can be to others is when we're at our best.

3. Give yourself permission to flourish. Of course you know others deserve to be happy, but you would need to decide that you also deserve the very best in life.

271
Men and Personal Development

In general, here are the three main fears that prevent men doing personal development work on their lives:

1. The fear of vulnerability. Exploring beneath the surface only risks exposing possible inadequacies.

2. The fear of appearing weak. Reaching out for help is a sign of weakness. A true man should be able to solve things alone.

3. The fear of being emotional. Being emotional is often linked with losing control, so true feelings must be suppressed.

Men overcome these fears by questioning and examining the true measure of strength and weakness, leading to the following discoveries:

1. To take off your mask and show up as you are, not as you want to be, is an act of true courage, not weakness.

2. Utilising the resources of others to fill gaps in your skill set is also an example of strength and stubbornly refusing help when you need it shows great weakness instead.

3. Emotional intelligence is also a clear sign of strength as it gives you a deep and rich capacity for self-awareness and personal growth.

272
Dealing with Shame

....

Shame is something many people struggle with on some level. The underlying thought process that drives all shame is this: If you really knew me, and what I've done, you'd think differently about me and reject me.

Therefore, there is only one way to really overcome shame. You have to plumb the depths of your own behaviour and understand exactly why you did it and what it means about you.

Is it because you're bad?

Is it because you're wrong?

Is it because you're not enough?

While it's typical to judge ourselves, and others by what we do, the truth is that we are not our behaviour. In fact, all behaviours (even the most negative ones) have positive intentions. We're simply trying to bring peace and comfort to ourselves.

All behaviour is an attempt to meet our core needs of certainty, variety, significance, love, contribution and growth. We don't do bad things because we're bad, we do bad things because we're needy.

Now this doesn't justify the behaviour, but it also doesn't change the fact we are inherently good, trying to do the best we know how.

The way out of shame is to face yourself in the mirror and still deeply love and accept yourself. It is to know exactly what you've done and why you did it — yet come out the other side still liking yourself.

273
Real Hope vs False Hope

Do you know the difference between real and false hope?

False hope is wishing things will get better but believing deep in your heart they won't ever improve. It's feeling you deserve more but knowing you're stuck with your lot in life.

Real hope, on the other hand, is simply a product of embracing 100% choice. The moment you live with the illusion of no choice and succumb to the victim mindset, hope evaporates because you're out of options to improve your situation. You have no control as well as a belief that you have no real choice in the matter.

Wanting, wishing, hoping and longing — all while managing a residual disappointment — is the experience of false hope. If you remain in this space for too long, it gets inside you and inevitably dials down your expectation of life.

Don't confuse yourself by thinking all hope is the same. The only way to live with genuine hope is to position yourself with abundant choice. Sure, you don't always get to choose what happens to you, but you do get to choose your response.

As long as you embrace real choice, it's impossible to ever feel hopeless again.

274
Endless Possibilities

When you have exhausted all possibilities, remember this: You haven't. (Thomas Edison[70])

Wow! What a great quote from a guy who definitely put this theory into practice on his way to developing the incandescent light bulb in spite of thousands of failed attempts.

Typically, people try things a handful of times before giving up and declaring something impossible, often saying they've tried everything.

Remember — feeling stuck in life is simply the result of living with the illusion of no choice. We each have 100% choice and therefore access to limitless options.

When things don't work out, what else could you do? What else? What else? What else?

The image of the divine inside each of us is our capacity to create and go on creating. Therefore, it's literally impossible to get backed into a corner where you're out of options. We're just too powerful, too resourceful and too creative for that to ever happen.

So, no matter what's not working for you right now, and how hopeless things seem, pick yourself up, make a few changes and have another crack. Who knows what else you'll discover in the process!

275
Seasons of Relationships

The hero's journey metaphor, by Joseph Campbell,[71] helps us understand that if we are truly committed to finding our calling or unique contribution in life, not everyone in our life is going to be able to make that journey with us.

This is an important distinction to understand, because if you believe that current friends must remain friends for life, then when these people become gatekeepers and resist your growth, you won't allow them to phase out of your life while you move on beyond them.

This truth makes it easier to not cling to historic friendships as though they are static and unchanging, but to allow people to pass in and out of your life as the seasons change.

Although it may come with pain and grief, sometimes friendships end and paths diverge. If you've made some kind of blood commitment to be connected together for the rest of your lives no matter what, you run the risk of limiting each other's growth.

If you're committed to living a meaningful life, you'll always have good people in your world. The key is to honour the season you're in and be ready for change when it comes — otherwise you may never become the hero in your own story.

276
Back Down When You're Wrong

Love him or hate him, Donald Trump certainly is an interesting character. One of the things he has shown about himself, however, is that he has no reverse gear. While he prides himself on being a man of action, I promise you that an inability to back down is a weakness rather than a strength.

Early in his presidency, he used the word 'covfeve' in a late-night Tweet. It's likely it was a simple misspelling of the word 'coverage', yet when quizzed about this the next day, he assured the world it was no mistake. Trump told reporters that 'covfeve' was actually a secret word that only he and a few Whitehouse officials understood — all while the whole world laughed.

See, if you're never wrong, it completely undermines all credibility and respect. The underlying belief which prevents people from backing down is this: If I've been found to have done wrong, it must mean I am wrong or no good. Being wrong exposes deep insecurity.

I'm not suggesting you fold like a pack of cards every time someone looks at you sideways, but it is essential to own your mistakes, apologise and back down quickly when you're wrong, without taking it personally.

Admitting your flaws is not a sign of weakness. In fact, it takes real courage and humility instead. Ultimately, a show of authenticity always gains you more respect.

277
Rome Wasn't Built in a Day

Here is a sobering thought I've found useful: When things are bad, they can always get worse. And, when things are good, they can always get better.

This thought helps prevent you from getting too carried away with a win, or a loss, in any one moment. I'm sure if you did a survey at any one point in your life, you could find plenty of things that are going well and plenty of things that are not.

When it comes to success and failure, it's essential to play the long game. It's almost impossible to assess the true success of any one moment, choice or experience while it's happening. The old saying is true: Rome wasn't built in a day.

You can't fail or succeed as a parent, friend, business owner or spouse in any one moment. You'll have good days and bad days. You'll make good choices and poor ones. You'll regret some stuff and be grateful for other things.

This means you really don't have to get it right all the time and getting it wrong some of the time won't be what defines you. At the end of the day, the point is to keep going, keep learning and keep developing your ability to make better decisions today than yesterday.

278
Handling Disappointment

How do you handle disappointment?

If you're going to do anything remotely worthwhile, disappointment is inevitable. In an attempt to avoid disappointment, however, most people end up lowering their expectations. In fact, if you believe some people, the best way to never get hurt is to have no expectations at all! Now while that is one possible way of avoiding pain, this strategy causes you to end up living with false hope. It's this feeling of constantly wishing for things to be better but knowing in your heart they never will be.

The challenge of life is to welcome and accept disappointment as a core part of the goal setting process while remaining ambitious and optimistic. It's crucial to resist the temptation to dial down your standards and desires. Feel the pain and anguish of disappointment without letting it get inside you and settling in your bones.

Every single person who's achieved anything of worth has gone through all kinds of setbacks and disappointments in the process. Thankfully, they didn't let it dampen their overall enthusiasm for what they dared to believe was possible.

Have you let disappointment stop you?

279
The Importance of Being Wrong

It turns out that being wrong is absolutely essential for all growth and change. Author, Mark Manson, suggests it's worth remembering that for any change to happen, you must be wrong about something. And until you're able to question yourself to find it, nothing will change.[72] Therefore, discovering where you're wrong is wonderfully useful for new levels of personal growth and self-improvement.

Often people attach their beliefs to their identity, which makes it almost impossible to admit they're wrong. Being wrong is then seen as a personal failure. However, the key is to hold on to your beliefs tightly and loosely at the same time, knowing it's impossible to be 100% right about anything and that your beliefs do not define you as a person.

Rather than clinging to the need to be right, the moment you realise you're wrong, you're able to let go of what's not working and upgrade it for a better way of thinking and living.

In the words of the great American writer, futurist and businessman, Alvin Toffler, 'The illiterate of the 21st century will not be those who cannot read and write, but those who cannot learn, unlearn and relearn'.[73]

What are you wrong about right now?

280
Dealing with Narcissists

In order for narcissistic behaviour to survive, it requires those who are being treating poorly to remain stuck in their insecurity. The only reason narcissists get away with such bad behaviour is because they can.

As confronting as this is, it means that if you want to overcome the toxic effects of narcissists in your life, rather than pointing the finger, you need to deal with your own insecurity first. Remaining the victim or the martyr provides protection from your deepest fears about yourself and encourages the bullying to continue.

The truth is that no one can ruin your life without your permission.

Narcissists are consumed with their own agenda and can only imagine a world where they get exactly what they want. Thinking about what's best for anyone else but themselves is the furthest thing from their mind. Therefore, it's ridiculous to expect them to behave better of their own accord. If they can have their cake and eat it too, why wouldn't they?

If you don't like their behaviour, stop tolerating it. End of story. Each of us is 100% responsible for training others how to treat us by what we allow and deny. All change starts with you.

281
The Fine Trap

Sir Richard Branson is certainly one the most successful entrepreneurs the world has ever seen. Listening to his interview on the Tim Ferriss podcast, in 2019, I was struck with the wisdom of his parting comments. As the conversation came to an end, he told the audience this:

You will almost certainly have more fun and success in life if you are willing to stick your neck out and have a go rather than just sitting back watching the fortunes of others who are prepared to stick their necks out. It won't always be fine — that's guaranteed. But nothing ventured is nothing gained.

Knowing things won't always be fine and not expecting them to be, seems to be a real key to success. In fact, the word 'fine' seems to be the real trap!

Fine is a nothing kind of word. It's bland, boring and colourless. Fine is middle of the road — safe. When someone asks me how I'm going, I make a point of answering honestly, even if they were just asking to be polite. The last thing I want to hear out of my own mouth is that things are fine.

There have been plenty of times when things have not been fine in my life and there has been pain, anguish and frustration instead. Yet it has been these times of not being fine that have caused me to address and confront issues and limiting thinking in my own life, which has then ultimately led to new seasons of growth and progress.

If everything is fine, then it's likely you're in denial or playing it completely safe. Fine is a trap. Avoid it at all costs.

282
How to Handle Pressure

One of the key things that determine your ability to grow and succeed in life will be how well you handle pressure.

A new machine is pressure tested before being released onto the market to see if there are any leaks or weaknesses under stress. This is done to make sure the machine can cope with extreme conditions so customers can be confident it won't fail you when they need it most.

What would happen if your life were pressure tested? Where would you leak or crack first? Here are three keys to help you increase your ability to handle pressure:

1. Expect it. Life is hard. Success is hard. Change is hard. The road less travelled is hard. In fact, all the worthwhile stuff in life is hard. But that's ok because you're stronger than you think. You have been designed well. If you expect things to be easy, you will suffer the moment they get difficult. If you expect things to be hard, when challenges show up you're on the front foot and ready for them.

2. Face up to life. Every time you face something hard and see it through, it strengthens you. Every time you run away, it weakens you.

3. Keep working through all limiting beliefs about yourself that disempower you or lead you to feel inadequate. These beliefs can be replaced with empowering ones that serve you to deal well with all of life's challenges.

283
Letting Go of Lack

One of the most constant human drivers and motivators is the need for more. Whether it's a product of culture or our evolution, it's undeniable that we feel the need to have more, do more and be more.

However, many people's experience of life is at extreme odds with this desire for more. They fear things will get worse, not better, and feel a strong sense of lack in every area of life instead.

The great paradox of abundance is that it's already all around us. We're surrounded by the abundance of life in every way without having to do anything. There's a flow of life in you and through you every time you draw breath. You're connected to this life with every cell in your body.

Therefore, the path to plenty is always the process of letting go of lack. You don't have to earn abundance, work for it or even get to the point of deserving it. Instead, it's about removing the beliefs that keep you blind to what is already true.

While this idea is profoundly simple, most people still avoid it because of the fear that, somehow, they don't deserve it.

Do you give yourself permission to access abundance or will you continue to hold yourself back and remain in a state of lack?

284
Different Forms of Happiness

I'm always fascinated how different people see and experience happiness and I just love learning the great wisdom on how to do life well. Famous psychologist, Martin Seligman,[74] suggests there are three different forms of happiness we can each pursue.

The first level he calls the 'Pleasant Life'. Here, you aim to have as much positive emotion as possible and learn the skills to amplify positive emotion. On this level, it's all about pursuing whatever makes you feel good now.

The next level is the 'Engaged Life'. Here, you identify your highest strengths and talents and recraft your life to use them as much as you can in work, love, friendship, parenting and leisure. This is all about creating a lifestyle that you're in control of and where you're able to get paid doing what you love.

Finally, the third stage is the 'Meaningful Life'. Here, you use your highest strengths and talents to belong to and serve something you believe is larger than the self. This is all about finding purpose greater than your own life. He suggests this is the greatest form of true happiness.

Which level of happiness are you striving for? Have you found a purpose greater than your own life, or does everything start and end with you?

285
Weak vs Strong Surrender

There are plenty of hard situations in life where things are just not working out how you'd hoped, and it becomes an option to give up.

So, when is it ok to give up and when is it not? When is it quitting? When is it being realistic? When is it evidence of fear, and when is it faith? When is it weakness and when is it strength?

The difference can appear to be quite subtle, but it really is massive. One will be a setback, the other will actually move you forward. The key is to know the difference between your internal wisdom voice as opposed to your fear voice.

Ask these three questions to differentiate between the two:

1. Is this a decision based on fear or love?

2. If I had nothing to prove or defend, what would I do?

3. Is this the end of a season or am I just getting started?

Sometimes, the most courageous thing you can do is close the door and walk away. And at other times, courage is all about sticking it out. The cool thing is you have to really listen to your heart to work out which is the right option for you.

286
Powerful Presuppositions – Part 1

A presupposition is a background belief that is assumed and accepted to be true. Here are four of the most powerful presuppositions of those who do life well:

1. People work perfectly. You are not broken. The results you're getting in every area of life are the exact results you've designed your system to create. Every behaviour is meeting a need and every strategy has a positive intention.

2. You love yourself. All self-protection is evidence of self-love. Change comes when you make peace with yourself and work with yourself rather than through conquering yourself.

3. Your body craves health. Health is the default. When you take the handbrake off and give yourself permission to flourish, health is where you end up. Sickness, ill health and excess weight are serving you by protecting you from what you're most afraid of.

4. You have 100% choice. You are exactly where you've chosen to be. You may not choose what happens to you, but you always choose your response.

Imagine what would be possible if you believed these things too?

287
Powerful Presuppositions — Part 2

Here are another four of the most powerful presuppositions of those who do life well:

1. You only do what works. Everything in your life that you tolerate and complain about, but don't change, MUST be working for you. If there really were no payoff or reward, you would have changed it already.

2. You are not a victim. We are sense-making creatures who go into the world and tell stories about our experiences. Life is not based on what happens to you but on the meaning you place on these events. You're not just an actor in the story of your life — you're the storyteller.

3. Your results are your own. You are 100% responsible for your results and your relationships. You're constantly training others how to treat you by what you allow and deny. While blame and excuse may make sense, they leave you with no power to change anything.

4. You get what you want. We each have the power to get what we really want. If you don't have it, part of you doesn't want it or isn't prepared to pay the price to get it.

Clearly this is a very different road map for life than most people are living from. What would happen if these statements were true for you too?

288
The Power of Being Vulnerable

For many people, it's as though keeping up the appearance of having it all together is the most important thing. Therefore, vulnerability is to be avoided at all costs. As long as you look like you're winning, who needs to know what's going on beneath the surface?

The fear is that if people see what's really going on underneath the surface, they'll reject you. This fear, of being found out as lacking, keeps people wearing smiles and playing games. All the while, they're dying on the inside.

The paradox of vulnerability is that by showing up as you really are, not as you'd like to be, you discover the path to get where you want to go. Vulnerability, therefore, is a demonstration of great strength rather than weakness.

As Brene Brown says:

Owning our story can be hard, but not nearly as hard as spending our lives running away from it. Embracing our vulnerabilities is risky but not nearly as dangerous as giving up on love and belonging and joy — the experiences that make us most vulnerable. Only when we are brave enough to explore the darkness will we discover the infinite power of our light.[75]

289
Self-permission

Here's why I'm convinced self-permission beats self-discipline as a motivation strategy every day of the week.

Self-permission is about making peace with yourself. It's recognising that all the parts of you — even the ones that feel like they're at war — actually want the same thing. Everything is driven from a sense of protection and love and wanting the best for you.

It's about valuing the beauty and gold that lies within you. It is to honour your own wisdom and intuition. It is to build great rapport between your conscious and subconscious so that you find a way to work with yourself rather than against yourself.

Self-permission is realising that, ultimately, you're the only one powerful enough to get in the way of your own dreams and hold yourself back. and you're the only one with the power to cause you to succeed.

It is to take the handbrake off and allow yourself to be successful. It is to stop hiding your light under a basket and conforming to how the world wants to you be. It is the willingness to fully show up in the world, in all your uniqueness, and to shine for all to see.

When you give yourself permission to flourish, there's nothing strong enough or big enough to get in your way.

290
The Five Guiding Principles of Highly Successful People

To succeed in life is actually quite easy because most people never will. You only have to do a few key things semi-consistently and it quickly separates you from the crowd.[76]

Here are five practices that make success inevitable.

1. Know what you want. Without a compelling vision for how you'd like your life to be, there's nothing strong enough to cause you to deal with your insecurities and overcome internal limitation.

2. Let go of self-judgement. You can't do self-judgement and self-awareness at the same time. Being hard on yourself actually produces no positive change in your life. Use curiosity and compassion instead.

3. Meet your needs internally rather than externally. Take 100% ownership of your value and worth rather than contracting it out to your world.

4. Be the storyteller. The truth is that you're not just an actor in a story written by someone else. You're the storyteller. If your life isn't the way you'd like it to be, change the script.

5. Develop rapport with self. Rather than trying to get ahead by fighting against yourself, build a great relationship between your conscious and subconscious to allow you to work with yourself instead.

291
Anxiety

Did you know that anxiety needs a story in order to survive? Therefore, the aim of the game is to live out of a story where being anxious makes no sense.

Contrary to popular opinion, anxiety is not a condition that you simply have to survive or endure. It doesn't come out of nowhere. You're not broken. What's more, the source of your anxiety is not strange, random or unknown. There's always a reason, an underlying belief, a fear or an insecurity that has created the anxiety response to something in your reality.

So, of course you're anxious. Not as a judgement, but simply to state that emotion always flows out of belief. What must you believe about your life, your situation or yourself in order to be anxious? If there was is no limiting belief, then it just doesn't make any sense to be anxious.

Using this approach always gives you the ability to gain self-awareness about the underlying story. With awareness always comes more choice. You can't change what you can't see.

What would you need to believe right now in order to feel calm, confident and in control of your results? Those who are living free from anxiety — what must they believe?

292
Be Here Now

One of the most difficult but important aspects of genuine personal development work is to come out of hiding and be prepared to be here — right where you are now.

Whether you should or shouldn't be here is entirely irrelevant. You are here. Until you face up to 'here', you can never get to 'there'. So often, people dwell on the past or hope for the future and avoid their current reality.

An honest acceptance of the state of play in every area of life is a wonderful gift to give yourself if you ever hope to improve the quality of your results in each of these areas. To make it even more interesting, your results are your results, so you're exactly where you've chosen to be.

While that is incredibly confronting, and maybe even offensive, it's entirely true. When you accept it, you're then able to make different choices and make the changes you desire. If you're where you've chosen to be, then you have the power to choose to be somewhere else.

293
Problems

Mark Manson says that one of the key conditions for happiness in life is solving problems.[77] Yet interestingly, the problem of solving one problem is also the creation of the next problem! So, there will always be more problems!

Therefore, a life well lived is not about pretending you have no problems, avoiding problems or even striving to attain a problem-free life. It will instead be found in creating a scenario where you enjoy the problems you're solving and keep growing as a person, so you continue to earn higher quality problems.

This means that at any given time, there will always be plenty of great things and plenty of challenging things in your life at the same time. We need the struggle. It's good for us. We build character, strength and resilience as we work out how to overcome challenges.

As a kid, I'm sure you saw a butterfly struggling to get out of its cocoon and were desperate to help out, only to have an adult tell you that without this struggle, its wings would be too weak to fly. Don't wish the hard stuff away. A life well lived is all about solving problems.

294
How to be a Pessimist

If you've ever wondered how to be a pessimist and get stuck in really negative cycles of thinking and living, psychologist Martin Seligman[73] clearly explains how you can do this with three key words.

1. Personalisation. The belief that I am at fault. That this event, experience or conversation means something is wrong or lacking with me. This wouldn't have happened if I were different or better.

2. Pervasiveness. The belief that an event will affect all areas of life. This event has the power to negatively spill over and affect other areas of our lives. Because one thing is no good, all things will end up being no good.

3. Permanence. The belief that the aftershock of the event will last forever. This is my lot in life and bad things will continue to define my existence. There's no way out of this cycle for me, so I need to come to terms with this and survive the pain of my life.

4. Learned optimism, on the other hand, runs a very different strategy.

295
How to be an Optimist

Martin Seligman teaches that optimists run a very different strategy from pessimists, using the same three words mentioned in the previous chapter.

1. Personalisation. Optimists blame bad events on causes outside of themselves, while being quick to internalise positive events.

2. Pervasiveness. Optimistic people compartmentalise helplessness. They never assume that failure in one area of life means failure in life as a whole. Optimistic people also allow the good events to brighten every area of their lives rather than just the particular area in which the event occurred.

3. Permanence. Optimistic people believe bad events to be more temporary than permanent, and bounce back quickly from failure. They also believe good things happen for reasons that are permanent. Optimists point to specific temporary causes for negative events.

The optimist's outlook on failure can thus be summarised as: What happened was an unlucky situation (not personal), and really just a setback (not permanent) for this one, of many, goals (not pervasive).

296
Yes and No

The Bible says:[79] 'Let your yes be yes and your no be no.' These are two very small, yet powerful, words that will determine so much about the destiny of your life.

Take a moment to evaluate exactly what you're saying yes to and what you're saying no to. Beyond that, who are you saying yes to? And who are you saying no to?

Rather than your yes being the reluctance to say no, or your no being the fear of saying yes, make a decision to be intentional about your yes and no and say them out loud and on purpose.

If you say yes to everything and everyone, you really are saying yes to nothing. If you can't say no to someone, then your yes means nothing. Yes only has meaning when we say it because we want to, not because we feel we like we have to.

It's common for people to have a 'to-do list', but how about a 'to-NOT-do list'? What things really need to be cut out of your life for good?

In order to flourish in life, the aim of the game is to create a life you don't need an escape from. This will largely be determined by what you are saying yes and no to.

Get very clear about how you'd like things to be, and then let your yes be yes and your no be no.

297
Just Like Me?

People ask me all the time: Do you know anyone who is as stuck as me but has found a way to overcome these challenges and move forward again?

And every time my response is: So how would it serve you for me to answer that question?

If I say no, that will confirm their fears that it's too hard, and they are too broken. If I say yes, they'll immediately be trying to work out how they are in fact different from the other person.

The only questions that really matter are: Do you want to change? Is it important to you? Are you willing to do whatever it takes? Great! Then be the first. Even if no one has found a way to get back in the game from the place you find yourself in, be the first.

The world is full of stuff that was once impossible. But someone thought it important enough to find a way to bring it into being even if no one had ever done it before.

Remember, necessity is the mother of all invention. When the why becomes big enough, the how takes care of itself. Get clear about what you really want and why you're no longer willing to live without experiencing this in your life. Then you'll discover what you're really capable of.

298
Your Part in the Mess

One of my favourite coaching questions is also one of the most confronting: So, what is your part in this mess?

It's always far easier to focus on how others have contributed to the situation you're in. Yet at the same time this means you avoid the painful reality of your own contribution to your results and relationships.

Blame is natural and fun, but it leaves you with no power. What's more, blame is always an escape from responsibility. If it's not your responsibility or your fault, you get to play the victim.

The common victim script is: Surely I have nothing to do with this. It's not my fault, I am not to blame and it's all happening to me. I'm the innocent victim in all this. Please feel sorry for me and understand how much it sucks to be me.

Change always starts with responsibility. As soon as you own your part in the messy situations of your life, you become empowered to improve them. It also helps you to see that you're actually not a victim at all.

The great news is that the moment you see that you created this mess, then surely you can clean it up too.

299
Breaking the Cycle of Cause and Effect

One of the most powerful pieces of self-development work you can do is to set yourself free from unhelpful cycles of cause and effect.

We are sense-making creatures, always attaching meaning to our experience of life. This leads us to believe that everything must mean something and that things always happen for a reason. 'This' must cause 'that' effect.

Here are some common examples

1. When I've been disciplined, good things happen in my life.

2. As I get older it's harder to stay healthy.

3. When I get a financial win, a loss is just around the corner.

These rules seem so true and real, but that's simply because you can point to examples of where these exact things have happened. That's just the way our brain works. We'll always find evidence for whatever we believe is true. Everything else gets filtered out.

It's all just story though. What if it's not true? What if there's no real link between these two things except in your mind. What if you could tell a different story and therefore get very different results?

What unhealthy cause and effect patterns do you need to disconnect?

300
The Importance of Embracing the Dark Side

Fully facing my darkest fears and seeing myself come out the other side has definitely been an incredibly important and profound experience of growth in my life.

So often we run away from our biggest fears. However, the only way to really overcome the things we're most afraid of is to sit with them, fully face the worst-case scenario and see yourself coming out the other side.

For me, it was: What if I'm not awesome? What if I'm just an average guy from Goulburn and no one really cares about what I say or do?

It literally took me three weeks to fully sit with this horrible possibility, yet I realised that if this was actually true, I could still find meaning in loving my family and enjoying my desire to read, write and speak about personal development ideas. Nothing would actually change about how I lived my life.

This instantly enabled me to get over myself and stop being so scared and needy. Ironically, the moment I was able to show up with nothing to prove or defend, it turned out that I was actually an excellent coach!

What terrifies you? Is it actually as scary as you imagine? The only way to find out is to see yourself experiencing the thing you fear most, then coming out the other side unscathed.

301
Seeking Validation

Human beings cannot survive without feeling a strong sense of significance, value and worth. As children, we naturally seek this validation from our parents and unconsciously employ one or both of them as the chief validators in our life.

Whether you're aware of assigning this role or not is irrelevant. The fact is that, at some point, you made your parents the ones with the power to say whether or not you mattered and, therefore, you had to play by their rules in order to gain acceptance and validation.

Some parents are better than others at giving, but while ever you have an external source of self-worth, it is never lasting. You never fully believe it and even if you do get what you're looking for, it lasts for such a short time before you're craving it again.

No matter who we are or what our story is, at some point we must all find a way to take the power back and work out how to tell ourselves that we're enough rather than depending on that from others.

This means firing your parents (or anyone else for that matter) from the role of chief validator in your life and reassigning that role to yourself. Fully becoming an adult means validating yourself.

302
People have Done More with Less

History is full of extraordinary tales of great achievements from people who had no right to succeed the way they did. They had every reason to hide or play it small yet chose to go big instead!

If you look around, I promise you can always find people who've done more than you with less than you have, and those who've done less than you with more than you have.

This is why comparison is always dangerous. The only person to compare yourself with is you. Are you doing the best you can with what you've been given? Are you running your own race? Are you committed to maximising your gifts and talents for the good of those around you?

Resist the urge to compare yourself with those who seem stronger, smarter or more gifted than you. Stop complaining about what you don't have. Stop looking around for someone else to make it happen for you.

There's only one of you, and we're all counting on you to bring the best you've got. If you do, I promise it will be enough.

303
Setbacks

When things get really hard and obstacles rise up against you, what's your internal response?

The only certainty we have in life is that nothing is certain! This means things won't always work out how you expected, and setbacks are guaranteed. Life is unfair. People will hurt you and let you down. You will fail and fall. Opportunities will be missed. Things will go wrong.

The cool thing about these setbacks is they give you a real opportunity to dig deep and build some character. Obviously, resistance training actually requires resistance. If it was easy all the time, you'd never build any muscle.

As the Japanese proverb says: Fall down seven times, stand up eight.

I've found that when your face is in the dirt, these two questions are the only things powerful enough to get you back up again: What do you really want? What are you prepared to do about it?

You're welcome to blame everyone and everything else about why things don't work out — or you can step up and find a way forward. Your results are yours.

304
Busyness = Laziness, and Laziness = Fear

Bestselling author and podcaster, Tim Ferriss, says that being over-scheduled and over-committed is a common part of the culture of busyness and work in today's world.

The default mode is always to do more. If I have a problem — do more. If I'm feeling stressed out — do more. While it might seem logical to increase output, Ferriss says that indiscriminate activity is a form of laziness.[80]

On a superficial level, being busy is a satisfying substitute for doing important work. It's very easy to confuse activity with productivity, yet the real question is: What is actually stopping you prioritising the most important work over just being busy and cramming your life full of non-essential work?

So, if busyness is actually laziness, it turns out laziness is merely a manifestation of fear. The reason you keep avoiding certain tasks and are unmotivated to finish some projects is because you're afraid. If you were to fully commit to your most important work and say no to everything else, then what if your best is not good enough and you fail?

Being busy is a clever hideout to prevent you from being found out as inadequate or somehow lacking. The issue is not busyness or laziness — it's fear.

305
Craving Certainty

Even though we all require a measure of certainty in our life, we crave this certainty in a very uncertain world. As such, it's useful to realise that the most resourceful form of certainty is to embrace uncertainty and then back yourself. The moment you need things outside of you to be a certain way to be ok, you're in trouble because, ultimately, you have no control. Who knows what tomorrow will bring?

Because this idea is so important, I wear two rings to help anchor me to this truth. The one on my left hand is a reminder of the commitment I made to my wife over 20 years ago and the certainty of my love for her, while the one on my right hand is a visual reminder of a commitment I made to myself around 10 years ago.

When I first discovered the paradox of needing certainty in an uncertain world, I knew I had to find this certainty internally instead. In that moment, I decided that the most certain thing I could do was to stop playing it safe and small and to give myself permission to step up and bring my 'A-game' to life.

Embracing uncertainty and backing myself meant eating well, dressing sharply, standing tall, owning my value, speaking my message and believing in my capacity to handle whatever situation I'm faced with. Although I never know what tomorrow will bring, I do know that I'll work it out when I get there, just like I have every other day of my life.

306
The Difference Between Blame and Responsibility

One of the questions I get asked most often is to know the difference between blaming yourself and taking responsibility for your results. Although these two approaches can appear very similar on the surface, they are in fact worlds apart in application.

Self-blame is a form of judgement designed to protect you from the judgement of others. If you attack yourself for the things you've done wrong, then no one else needs to. The intention of self-blame is not to change the situation but to protect yourself from others blaming you by getting in first.

The intention of responsibility, on the other hand, is always to make things better. All change starts and ends with responsibility. It is to accept your place in this mess and own your power to do things differently.

There's no judgement in responsibility. There's no personal praise or criticism within responsibility. It separates behaviour from intention. Responsibility is so much cleaner than blame. It allows you to assess why you made the past choice, extract the key learning and feel empowered to make different choices in the future.

307
Your Job is Supposed to Suck

Did you know that after a while your job is supposed to suck? If you were to stop and ask the first 10 people you came across today to tell you about their jobs, I'll guarantee you'll hear some painful stories.

Most people do not love their work. They often experience high levels of stress, frustration and pain around their employment situation. The interesting news is that while being in the workforce as a responsible adult is a really healthy thing for a season, after a while your job is supposed to suck.

Pain is guaranteed. In fact, it's actually normal, healthy and to be entirely expected that you will grow to hate your day job. Sooner or later, working for the man is going to create major pain in your life. There's nothing surer.

Now, rather than this being a huge problem, it's actually a wonderful thing. The pain is there to let you know that it's time to keep growing. It's time to find your voice and your sweet spot, and step beyond the comfort of the system into the realm of the entrepreneur. This allows you to create a lifestyle around doing work that you enjoy, are good at and something that gives you the ability to leave your unique mark on the world.

Each one of us has a contribution to make that can never fully be achieved by serving someone else's vision.

308
Why People Don't Listen to Their Pain

If pain is our most honest and loving voice, why do most people avoid listening to what their pain is telling them? The fear is that you can't afford to listen because your pain is going to ask something impossible of you.

You might be suffering at work, but if you were to listen to your pain it would tell you that this job is killing you and you need to find something else. The issue is you don't know what else you could possibly do.

Or, you may be super stressed and run down, but if you were to stop and listen to your pain, it would tell you to get more sleep and take a holiday. The problem is you can't see how that's possible with the things required of you.

Your relationships with your kids may be getting increasingly distant. You hate what's happening but if you were to actually listen to your pain it would tell you that there are some urgent conversations to be had. The problem is you don't have any idea how to have them.

Pain is a gift from God, designed to protect you from future and worse pain. Because pain is a loving voice, it wouldn't be telling you to take action unless you were actually up to the task, despite all your doubts and fears. Yes, it's hard to listen but it's always worth it.

309
Life is Suffering

Even a brief scan of the history of humanity and an exploration of the lives of the people we admire show that, in actual fact, life is suffering. While that sounds incredibly bleak and pessimistic, it has been one of the most liberating discoveries of my life.

If you want to fix your marriage, you'll face suffering, but if you don't fix it, you'll still suffer.

The path to business success is full of suffering, but you'll also suffer greatly if you're too scared to start your business.

To face your fears will cause suffering but to let them consume you will also create huge suffering.

If you desire to train for a marathon, you'll suffer, but if you sit on the lounge and never push your body, you'll still end up suffering.

We get transformed through our suffering when we choose the right kind.

Mark Manson says:

If suffering is inevitable, if our problems in life are unavoidable, then the question we should be asking is not 'How do I stop suffering?' but 'Why am I suffering and for what purpose?'[81]

Our mission is to choose suffering that's meaningful rather than suffering for nothing.

310
Nesting in Your Hair

The great 16th century protestant reformer, Martin Luther, said: 'You can't stop birds flying around your head, but you can stop them nesting in your hair.'

Over the years, I've found this to be such life-giving advice. The direct application of this idea from Luther has to do with the abundance of crazy thoughts, ideas and temptations that pop into our heads from time to time. Who knows where they come from, or why these thoughts show up, but the point is that while we all experience head noise, we can choose not to let them take root in our minds.

We are not our thoughts. They're just impulses and suggestions. We don't need to take them all seriously and we definitely don't have to indulge or act on them.

I think it's common for people to freak out about the crazy thoughts they have and feel it proves there's something really wrong with them. Yet there's no point judging yourself for something you have no control over.

See the thought come in and see it go out again. It doesn't have to stay, and it doesn't have to mean anything. You can't stop the birds flying around your head, but you can definitely stop them nesting in your hair!

311
Productivity

Peter Drucker, father of modern management theory, believed people are effective *because* they say no.

In his fantastic book, *Essentialism*, Greg McKeown tells the story of Drucker's wastepaper basket strategy to maximise his productivity. His reply to Hungarian professor Mihaly Csikszentmihalyi, best known for his revolutionary work on flow state, is one of the most provocative and extraordinary statements on the subject I've ever come across. It has been lodged firmly in my head ever since I read it. In fact, it's one of the very reasons I've been able to prioritise this book long enough for you to actually be reading it now!

Drucker says:

I am greatly honoured and flattered by your kind letter of February 14th—for I have admired you and your work for many years, and I have learned much from it. But, my dear Professor, I am afraid I have to disappoint you ... I hope that you will not think me presumptuous or rude if I say that one of the secrets of productivity is to have a very big wastepaper basket to take care of all invitations such as yours—productivity in my experience consists of not doing anything that helps the work of other people but to spend all one's time on the work the good Lord has fitted one to do, and to do well.[82]

What is the work the good Lord has fitted you to do? What does that mean saying no to, to make sure you are as productive as possible in that work?

312
Change is Hard

I often get asked why change is so hard. I respond the same way every time — it is supposed to be!

It's hard because it's valuable and beautiful and worthwhile. If it were easy, we wouldn't have reason to celebrate it. Real, meaningful change isn't complicated but it's definitely not easy either. It's always simple and hard.

The road less travelled is called that for a reason. It's in no danger of being trampled and overrun by the masses. Most people won't ever find a way to change the things about their life that they don't like. Why? Because it's hard. They'll continue to do what is safe, comfortable and easy.

The most interesting thing about the avoidance of what appears to be hard is that it creates its own experience of pain and suffering that becomes incredibly hard to endure.

So, change is hard. Yep, we get that. But so is staying the same!

Therefore, if it's true that both the road less travelled and the highway of mediocrity are hard, you may as well choose the hard that's actually going to be meaningful and connected to your sense of purpose in life rather than hiding or playing it safe.

313
One-minute Manager

The One-Minute Manager, by Ken Blanchard, still rates as one of the highest selling business books of all time, and for good reason. One of the greatest challenges in managing and leading people is often how personal it all becomes, yet Blanchard's wisdom on the subject overcomes that challenge by separating a person's behaviour from the person themselves.

Using the simple framework of one-minute goals, one-minute praise and one-minute reprimands, allows you to communicate in a very clean and clear manner within groups, teams or even families.

One-minute goal setting is about being aware of what's expected from the beginning. Decide on the desired goal; keep it simple, communicate it clearly and don't change it. There is nothing more demoralising for teams than unclear goals or moving goalposts.

The aim of one-minute praise is to catch people doing something right, in line with the stated goal. The emphasis is to acknowledge the thing they did as soon as you notice it, not to comment on them as a person because you've already established that they're a good person separate from what they do or don't do.

Finally, one-minute reprimands are given as soon as something does not align with the agreed goal. Again, it's aimed at the work and not the doer. When someone behaves in a way that's not in alignment, they're never blamed as a person.

314
Self-deception

American physicist, Richard Phillips Feynman, famously said: 'The first principle is that you must not fool yourself — and you are the easiest person to fool.'[83]

So how do you know if you're deceiving yourself? Here are three ways of checking whether there's any self-deception in your life.

1. Are you pretending not to know? Wherever you hear yourself respond to the same question by saying 'I don't know' at least three times, there's a good chance you actually do know, and you're just pretending not to so you don't have to deal with it.

2. Are you hiding in plain sight? The best place to hide is always where no one thinks you are hiding — not even you. Carrying an extra 5 to 10 kilos is one of the best hideouts that exist. Mediocrity, busyness and blending in are other examples.

3. Are you obfuscating? That's a fancy word for clouding or confusing the issue. This happens when you talk your way out of taking responsibility. It's a form of self-deception because you get to sound intelligent, thought through and across the detail. All the while, you're avoiding facing the truth of the situation.

All self-deception is fear-based. We're just afraid of being exposed and found out as lacking and inadequate. Ultimately, the way out of self-deception is to face the irrational fears about ourselves.

315
Purpose

Finding your life's purpose can be difficult. I find it useful to start with what the answer isn't and work my way back from there.

Your purpose is NOT to try to inspire others. While lots of social media influencers orient their whole message around drawing attention to their achievements and triumphs over adversity with the stated intention of inspiring others to do the same, no one is actually inspired by these displays of attention-seeking and ego.

Your purpose is NOT to prove other people wrong. People do all kinds of remarkable things, purely motived by the haters, naysayers and doubters who've all told them they can't or won't. Yet when the seemingly impossible achievement is reached, they're often no more fulfilled than when they began. Surely true purpose has to be bigger and more beautiful than that?

It CANNOT be your purpose to prove that you matter. Your work is to discover your inherent worth separate from what you do or have, or what anyone else thinks of you.

Then you can go into the world with your cup full and with something of value to give. You are now free to make a contribution out of the essence of who you are, and connect with a purpose that's bigger than you and not about you.

316
Fully Becoming an Adult

One of the simplest ways to understand genuine personal development is that it's the journey of fully becoming an adult.

The definition of adulthood is self-sufficiency and the key role of every parent is to prepare their children for adulthood. However, most parents only focus on developing their child's physical and financial self-sufficiency, while the idea of emotional, relational and intellectual maturity is often completely overlooked. This means most people grow up physically, while remaining childlike, dependent and needy in many other areas.

The key to a meaningful and fulfilling life is to fully become an adult. It is hard but important work and there's no way around it.

Here are three central components of adult life:

1. Take full responsibility for your response to life rather than being a victim of what others say and do to you.

2. Meet your needs for love, significance and certainty internally rather than externally while being fully self-sufficient.

3. Be clear about exactly what you want and be willing to do what's necessary to make it happen.

The great news is that every cell in your body is on a trajectory towards maturity and is designed for adulthood. It's the natural order of things, and it's only doubt, fear and insecurity that leaves us clinging to childish ways.

317
Go Back Before Moving Forward

....

To untangle the messy stories of lack, limitation and insecurity, it's essential to go back to the start, where these stories were created in the first place. This means you've got to go backwards first before you can really move forward in your life.

Most people try and deal with the mess in their head by pretending it doesn't exist, or through self-medication and various coping strategies. It often seems too painful and overwhelming to try and untangle the mess or get to the bottom of things, therefore the only remaining option is to distance yourself from your past and survive the impact it's had on your life.

Yet, without going back to where that limiting story was first created and deconstructing it all the way back to the start, you'll inevitably continue to live out of that very story as the defining narrative in your life.

Until you go back and review the data around your past choices and experiences, and the way you've made sense of what these experiences say about you, you'll be eternally impacted by them. Lasting change and true freedom comes only through fully reconciling the past while firmly positioned as the storyteller, not the victim or the actor in a story written by someone else.

318
Reviewing Your Story

Here are five key ideas to help you do the real work of reviewing and rewriting your limiting beliefs today:

1. Accept that all we have is story. We are sense-making creatures who go into the world and tell stories to give meaning to our experiences. It's all just a story though. It's all a work of fiction. There are a multitude of other stories that could be told about the same experience. Each story leads to a very different destination.

2. Become aware of your particular story. Do this by simply observing your patterns of behaviour. Behaviour never lies. It always flows out of our beliefs. Then ask: 'What MUST I believe in order to behave this way?'

3. Trace the story back to the very beginning. When was the first time you told yourself this was true? What exact event, experience or conversation did you personalise negatively?

4. Realise there was a time in your life before this story was true for you. This means the story you're living out of is not you. It's an addition to your life — not actually who you are.

5. Take responsibility for the fact you're not just an actor in the story, but the storyteller. If you don't like the stories you've told about your life to this point, you and only you can go back and write new ones.

319
Freedom Poem

The way we speak to ourselves is a huge part of what gets programmed into our hearts and becomes the script we live out of. After discovering the power of self-talk, I'm very intentional about speaking to myself in a way that's empowering, enlarging and calls me into life and love.

Here is a poem I wrote to myself that has become particularly useful. Perhaps it will be useful to you too?

There is no fear of loss,
because I cannot lose and even if I could, I have nothing to lose.
There is no fear of failure,
because failure does not exist.
If I don't win, I learn.
There is no fear of isolation,
because separation is an illusion.
I am deeply connected to all life around me.
There is no fear of lack,
because abundance is all around me.
Life is abundant.
There is no fear of inadequacy,
because I have always been enough and always will be.
I deeply love and accept myself.
There is no fear of losing control,
because having control is a myth.
I will embrace uncertainty and back myself.
The sun will go on shining with or without me.
The earth does not need my say so in order to keep spinning.
There is no fear of sustaining success,
there is nothing to sustain.
My success is not mine to cling to.
I am merely a channel for the abundance of God.

320
The Adult Question

'What do you want?' is the ultimate adult question. It's the question children desire but are not ready for, and the one adults are ready for but would rather avoid.

As a parent, there's no way you're going to fully trust your kids to make every decision in their life based on what they do or don't want. If you let them swing away, they'd want junk food, inappropriate TV shows, late nights and no school! Instead, as a responsible and loving parent, you take this question off the table and tell them to trust and obey you instead, so they don't ruin their lives.

Yet, by the time the child has grown up and become an adult and is now the chief decision maker in their own life, most end up giving the adult question back for fear of getting it wrong or making a mistake.

I talk to lots of young adults who seem to have no idea what they really want for their life. The problem is, if you're not clear about what you want, the only other possible outcome is to find yourself serving the agenda of the people who do. That's how the world works.

The aim of the game is to grow up and fully become an adult. This means the *'what do you want'* question has to become a central point of focus.

Yes, it's difficult and dangerous. Yes, it exposes you to all kinds of potential failure, disappointment, judgement and conflict. But the moment you shut the question down as an adult, you remain like a child.

321
Reconciling Disappointment

One of the unavoidable costs associated with being ambitious is the disappointment, pain and frustration of not achieving what you set out to do.

I'm sure it's possible to live in a space of true presence where you're able to simply accept what 'is' without needing it to be different. Yet until you've truly broken through into the realm of having no expectations, you will suffer when things don't happen the way you'd like them to.

For the average person, pretending to have no expectations is simply a form of fatalistic defeatism to protect yourself from pain. To desire is human. This means to shut down desire is to dehumanise yourself.

Therefore, disappointment is actually a normal and healthy part of the human experience. Our responsibility is to reconcile it before it creates residual pain and reduced capacity for hope and future goal setting.

If the disappointment is allowed to linger, you'll have already unconsciously answered the two unavoidable questions negatively: Why did this happen and what does it mean about me?

Aim high and accept the disappointment when it comes, but make sure you choose a meaning that keeps you aiming high in the future.

322
Internal Representation

Reality is made up only by our internal representation system. We experience the world through our senses and then have to interpret and decode the input. Imagination. Meaning. Story.

When I say 'baked beans' for instance, you instantly have an internal experience of what baked beans means to you. Perhaps you love them. Maybe you hate them. Possibly they're connected with flatulence or being good for your heart.

The point is everyone has their own pictures, feelings or thoughts about those two words. So even though baked beans are real and have their own objective qualities, we experience them subjectively. This means baked beans are entirely different for every single person.

Now, obviously this is not just true for baked beans, but for everything we encounter. One person loves goal setting and finds it easy. The next person feels pressure and frustration when they hear that idea and therefore resist setting goals.

The problem is not goal setting, but our internal coding for what goal setting means to us. As soon as we understand this idea, it means we have the ability to change our internal experience with anything. Even baked beans!

323
Be Impeccable with Your Word

Don Miguel Ruiz's book, *The Four Agreements*, had a profound impact on me when I first read it on a flight to Melbourne. It's full of such wonderful wisdom and beautifully explains the fact that it's the agreements we make that ultimately shape our lives.

When you come to terms with this one idea, it's life changing! This means no one has the power to bless us or curse us with their words without our permission. It is to understand that it's not the harsh, unkind or cruel words said about us that diminish us, only the words we agree with.

It's not that the teacher said that you'd never amount to anything — it's that you agreed with those words. It's not that your dad said you were beautiful and incredible — it's that you agreed with him.

It's these agreements you make with words that have the real power. It's your own opinion of yourself that really determines what you become.

Ruiz says the first agreement we need to make is to be impeccable with our word. This means never use words against yourself or others. Never agree with anything that diminishes you and never speak words that diminish others.

324
Less to More

One of my favourite tests to run on change strategies is to make sure they are a 'less to more' transaction. Unless the desired change feels like you're actually getting a better deal in the real world, the change will never stick.

Remember we're entirely motivated away from pain and towards pleasure. So, if change feels like more to less — you feel like you really should stop it, cut it out, give it up, grow up, be better, try harder — then subconsciously it feels like you'll end up with less than you currently have. That is never sustainable.

There are two simple ways of creating a less to more transaction:

1. Do an accurate and thorough cost analysis of the downsides of your current reality. Are you actually pretending that staying here is better than it really is?

2. Gamify the change — create fun, adventure and reward into the desired change so it's linked with as much pleasure as possible. Until it actually feels like less to more — like you're going to get a better deal by making the change — you're fighting against yourself to win.

Less to more not only makes the change easy, but inevitable. Every cell in your body is now working with you to achieve the desired result.

325
Start with 'Who?'

When faced with a difficult decision about the way forward from where you are now to where you ultimately want to be, there are five questions you can ask to solve the problem:

1. What do I need to do?

2. How am I going to do it?

3. Why is this important to me?

4. When will I get it done?

5. Who do I need to help me?

Interestingly, the order you ask these questions will determine the speed in which you resolve the issue, if at all.

The slowest path forward is always via the *how* questions. *'How am I going to do it?'* often leaves you paralysed with uncertainty and fearfully overwhelmed all because you don't know how, and you'll need to reinvent the wheel to figure it out.

What and *when* are slightly better questions, however, asking *why* speeds up the process dramatically. In fact, when the why becomes big enough, the how takes care of itself.

The fastest path is always via the *who*. Who has solved this problem in the past that I can model? Who has the skills, tools, frameworks and processes I'm lacking right now? Who can show me the how?

Which order are you asking these questions? See what happens when you switch it around.

326
What is Wisdom?

Israel's King Solomon, referred to as the wisest man who ever lived, said we should seek wisdom above all else, like it's a precious treasure.[84]

In order to really solve significant issues in your life, you always need to encounter true wisdom.

So, what is wisdom and how do you differentiate it from the cheap substitutes? True wisdom is the intersection of these three things.

1. Wisdom is spiritual. It is always universal and ancient. There are threads of wisdom in the stories and traditions of those who've gone before us. No one owns wisdom, they're merely channels or vessels.

2. Wisdom is practical. It is always simple, complete and intelligent. Wisdom is never abstract or aloof.

3. Wisdom is transformational. The Bible says: 'Wisdom is known by her children.'[85] That is, wisdom always produces fruit. True wisdom leaves a mark, changes the game and creates lasting transformation.

Seek wisdom like your life depends on it because it actually does.

327
Getting Your MEDS Right

Positive psychologist, Ellen Jackson,[86] says the *MEDS* acronym is such a useful way of thinking about a baseline for mental health. Mindfulness, Exercise, Diet and Sleep are four simple and practical elements of not only a healthy body but more importantly, a healthy mind.

Mindfulness, Exercise, Diet and Sleep are no longer optional extras for superheroes with lots of time and money. This is par for the course. If you're not getting your MEDS, you're almost certainly in survival mode. All your energy is invested in not dying. Running your life on survival mode renders all efforts and tasks incredibly inefficient. It leaves you with no energy for problem solving and growth.

If you're struggling with mental health right now, focusing on basic movement, good sleep, healthy meals and some simple mindfulness really will make a significant difference! It's incredible how dark the world can be when these things are neglected.

Focusing on MEDS is not an issue of forcing yourself to do the things you don't want to do but treating yourself with loving kindness. Avoiding these four essential elements is short-sighted and quite cruel.

Are you getting all your meds?

328
Thinking New Thoughts

Research into typical brain activity suggests that about 98% of the thoughts we have each day are the exact same thoughts we had the previous day!

The issue is that if you keep thinking exactly the same thoughts every day, it makes sense to expect the exact same results every day.

The amazing thing is that creativity — or bringing into existence that which is completely new — is evidence of the divine inside each of us! So, to have no new thoughts means you have suppressed who you really are and what you're really capable of.

So how do you have new thoughts? Here are a few key ideas:

1. Expose yourself to new learning through books or podcasts.
2. Get outside your own thought life through meditation or mindfulness exercises.
3. Ask high-quality questions.
4. Meet new people.
5. Try new things.
6. Step outside what is safe, known and comfortable.
7. Journal daily.
8. Listen to your dreams.
9. Set aside thinking time.

Thinking new thoughts are an essential element of growth and self-improvement.

329
Changing Your Partner

When it comes to marriage or romantic relationships, I'm sure you've heard it said that you are to love your partner for who they are and that it's wrong to try and change them.

I don't buy it. In fact, I think this is possibly some of the worst relationship advice ever given. The truth is that if you don't find a way to change your partner, they'll annoy the life out of you, and you'll end up hating them. I promise that wasn't what you had in mind when your relationship started.

Most marriages descend into a convenient arrangement for this very reason — because no change happens.

Here are a few keys to change your partner and let them change you.

1. Keep focused on what you really want together. What's your dream for the relationship? Beginning with the end in mind and working your way back from there always helps you realise that if you stop growing, you'll never get to this goal.

2. Realise that love is motivated by the highest good for someone else. To love your partner, therefore, is to be part of their journey towards their best self.

3. Take the plank out of your own eye first so you can clearly see the speck in their eye. Always be willing to deal with your own stuff first before you address the faults and weaknesses in your partner.

330
Dress Like Today is Important

One of the quickest ways to change your state is to change what you're wearing. I've experimented with this idea a lot over the last 10 years. I love how powerful it is and I love how most people dismiss it as not important at all. This means it's super easy to get an unfair advantage in life by being willing to swim against the flow.

I approach the issue of what I wear with these two questions:

1. What outcome am I aiming to achieve?

2. Who would I need to be to get what I want?

Rather than asking what I need to do, I've learnt the power of focusing on 'being' first. I then dress accordingly.

Dressing intentionally clearly helps to remind me who I'm being. The coach? The entrepreneur? The dad? The husband? The mate? The athlete? The author? The farmer? The recluse? Great! Then dress properly for the role. If I show up in the wrong way for the outcome I'm trying to achieve, then I'll never be successful.

You may think you're just one person and may only have one wardrobe style. A simple review of the number of roles you really have and the goals you've set for each role reveals that by not dressing in character, you're showing up all wrong.

Greet each new day as if it's important. Dress like it matters and the day is a gift to you that you're ready to embrace with your best energy.

331
Review Your Agreements

The stories we live out of can be described as the things we've consciously and unconsciously agreed to. These agreements shape the entire course of our life and affect every experience we have.

People who succeed in life do so largely based on the fact they tell better stories than everyone else and therefore have made more empowering agreements.

In order to make deep and lasting change, it's essential to review the agreements you've made and decide if they're still working for you. Put simply, your life is shaped by what you say yes and no to. Being clear about these decisions is essential to being where you are on purpose.

To do this exercise most effectively only requires you to be mindful about what you're saying yes to. A strong yes is actually displacing the need to be clear about what you're saying no to. For example, if you're saying yes to showing up at your best, where it matters most, then by default you've already said no to hiding, blaming and playing small.

How often do you review your current agreements? What are you saying yes to today? What powerful agreements will shape your future?

332
Set Clear Intentions

The most famous words of Roman emperor and stoic philosopher, Marcus Aurelius, still ring true almost 2,000 years after he penned them.

Our actions may be impeded, but there can be no impeding our intentions or dispositions. Because we can accommodate and adapt. The mind adapts and converts to its own purposes the obstacle to our acting. The impediment to action advances action. What stands in the way becomes the way.

This is the importance of setting clear intentions. Things rarely work out the way you think they will and, as Aurelius says, obstacles get in the way and our plans get stopped. However, when you're crystal clear about your intentions, then you'll always find a way. When your why becomes big enough, the how takes care of itself.

Setting intentions for what you want to have happen helps you know exactly how to show up. It also enables you to connect with the abundance of internal and external resources available to you to get more of what you want.

How clear are your intentions for every area of your life?

333
Problem-solving Questions

Here are my three favourite problem-solving questions:

1. What problem are you most looking to solve right now? This sounds simple, but you can't fix it until you've named it. Be precise. What specifically is wrong? One of the biggest challenges to solving problems in our lives is that we often haven't understood what the problem actually is.

2. Are you sure that's actually the problem? Be careful you're not just dealing with the symptoms of a deeper problem. Most people are full of self-judgement for having the problem in the first place, which clouds their ability to accurately understand the true problem. Misdiagnosis instantly stops the problem-solving process. It means you waste time, money and energy on the wrong thing.

3. Who would know how to solve this? Who has already solved this exact problem before? What would they say to you? Modelling an expert allows you to avoid having to start from scratch and recreating the wheel. As Einstein says: 'You can't solve the problem with the same level of thinking that created it in the first place.'

334
Review Questions

One of the patterns of successful people is that they frequently stop and review their current position to make sure it's in line with their desired outcomes. Developing a rhythm of life that includes regular reflection and reviews the direction and current status of your life is an essential part of effective course correction.

Here are six of my favourite review questions:

1. What treasure do you seek?

2. Are you sure that's what you really want?

3. Do you have the right map?

4. Who can help show you the way?

5. What are you willing to sacrifice to get there?

6. Are you sure?

High-quality questions will always open up new paths in your mind. And new paths always lead to new destinations.

If this does not come naturally to you, then asking yourself these questions is a great place to start. If you're already comfortable with this, then giving someone else permission to regularly ask you these questions takes it to a whole new level as it's much harder to get away with answers that aren't true.

335
You are Not the Victim — You are the Persecutor

The quickest and most effective way to step out of the victim space is to realise you're not a victim at all. You need to see that you are, in fact, the persecutor. However, as Don Miguel Ruiz says, it's not the cruel words spoken to us that ruin us, it's only the words we agree with.[87] Therefore, you are the real bully in the story!

The battle has always been with your own opinion of yourself. You're the one who created the insecurity, and therefore you're the only one who can change it.

While you remain convinced that others have ruined your life, you inadvertently place all your hope for change on these same people fixing your problems too. You end up powerless, waiting for people to do things they're probably incapable of.

People often spend so much energy being upset at those who've wronged them, longing desperately for them to make it right. Yet all along, you've been the one who's done the damage. This means you're the only one who can make it right.

You're actually the one who needs to apologise, not the one who's waiting for the apology. Fancy that!

336
The Subject-Object Switch

Harvard psychologist, Robert Kegan argues that the subject-object switch is the single most important move we can make to accelerate personal growth.[88]

Being subjective about our experience is a natural and wonderful part of being a human being. Our experiences are precisely that — ours!

The issue is that while we're inside these experiences, we have no ability to change them. It's only as we step outside our own filters, perception and cognitive bias, and gain distance from our subjective experience, that we gain the ability to adjust the lens.

Stephen Covey says this ability to be self-aware and to think about our thinking is what most distinctly differentiates us from animals.[89]

Every moment spent being objective about the choices we're making always gives us more awareness and more choice. When we have more choice, we naturally make better choices. It's the illusion of no choice, characterised by being in the subject space, that leaves us feeling stuck.

Practising the subject-object switch therefore becomes an essential skill to develop if we want to improve the quality of our life.

337
What is Your Quest?

Connecting to meaning and purpose that's bigger than you is one of the most effective ways of not being held back by fear or lack of confidence.

It seems the most confident and self-assured people are those who see their life as an integral part of something bigger than them. This quest serves to make sense of their life when nothing else does.

Being driven and compelled by a purpose outside you, that is bigger than you, and actually not even about you, leaves very little room for you to worry about whether you're good enough.

The good news is that discovering your purpose in life is far less dramatic than most people imagine. All that's really required is for you to accept the call to adventure. You never really know where it will take you at the time, but you understand it will lead you somewhere bigger and more meaningful than your ordinary life.

As the 13th century poet, Rumi, so beautifully says: 'What you seek is also seeking you.' This means every time you open yourself to life and say yes to the adventure, you inevitably get closer to a life of true meaning and purpose.

338
Out of Fear and Into Process

Irrational fear feeds off uncertainty. It thrives in the space where you don't know what to do. Therefore, in every case, the way out of fear is always into process. This means you have to trust the process.

Whether it's rock climbing, business development, driving a car, buying a new house, getting married, learning to dance or starting a job at McDonalds, find someone who has zero fear about the thing you're terrified about and you'll notice that they have a well-worked process they're completely confident in.

If you allow them to take you through the process they use, you'll come out the other side completely fine. To have someone with the ability to take you out of story and into process, and help, is an essential part of the process of eradicating any fear.

Have a look at the things you're overwhelmed with right now, and you'll notice a lack of process. Find the process and the fear disappears.

339
Practice 1 – Step into the Light

While most people think personal insecurity is something you have to live with and manage for your entire life, I'm convinced that it's a problem that can definitely be solved. There are seven essential practices for doing this work.[90] Practice number one is to step into the light.

It's really common to feel insecure about being insecure. Yet, at some point you've got to face up to the fact that it's true. Until you accept your current reality, lasting change is not even an option.

In the words of Yoda: 'Named must your fear be before banish it you can.' Practice 1 is to come out of hiding and name your deepest fear. It is to own that you're not actually afraid of failure or rejection, but the personal implications of these things. The real fear is that if you were to fail or be rejected, you'd be found out as somehow lacking, inadequate or not enough.

The key here is to see that the deepest fear is always your own opinion of yourself. This is exactly why this process is so exciting. Opinions can be changed — especially when they're your own.

Fear unexamined always grows. The moment you turn to face your fear, and examine its true nature, the fear is greatly diminished. Insecurity is always built on a work of fiction, yet until you come out of hiding and step into the light, it's impossible to begin the work of deconstructing this story to rewrite a new one.

340
Practice 2 – Take 100% Responsibility

In overcoming my own insecurity, the single most important idea was this: All insecurity is built on a work of fiction. I imagined that I felt inadequate and insecure because of all the negative things said and done to me. In my mind, these experiences proved there was some lack inside me or that I was somehow not enough. Yet, the game-changing discovery was that I was not the actor in the story written by someone else, I was the storyteller.

Once you define the problem accurately as your own opinion of yourself, Practice 2 is about owning your part in forming these opinions in the first place. We're sense-making creatures who go into the world and tell stories about why things happen and what they mean about us. It's these stories that form our opinions of ourselves. This means we created the insecurity problem, and we're the only ones who can fix it. We're already 100% responsible.

People often imagine the insecurity problem was created outside of them, so naturally they also look outside of themselves for the solution. But when you realise that you created your own insecurity, then you realise you're the only one who can uncreate it.

All change starts and ends with responsibility. It immediately takes you out of the victim space into the place of personal power.

341
Practice 3 – Stack the Pain

Just because you're insecure doesn't mean you have to pay attention to the real impact it's having on your life. Most people suppress pain in their life because they don't want to feel it, yet in doing so they miss a massive opportunity to access deep internal motivation for lasting improvement.

Stacking the pain involves running an accurate cost assessment of all the ways unresolved insecurity is ruining your life. Eradicating insecurity requires you to stop pretending everything is fine, or feeling this way is normal, and to face the truth about how much pain really is beneath the surface and caused by your low opinion of yourself.

Pain is designed to move us away from danger and towards safety. It's an essential part of the motivation for all change work. Whatever we link pain to, we naturally want to move away from.

Therefore, when you stack the pain of being insecure rather than ignoring it, your motivation for action peaks in a way where you'll be willing to do whatever it takes to never feel this way again. This creates a threshold moment where the pain of change becomes less than the pain of staying the same.

Practice 3 is all about feeling this pain as strongly as possible and letting it lovingly serve you as it was designed to do.

342
Practice 4 — Develop a Compelling Life Vision

Pain avoidance is only half the required motivation to sustain lasting change. While being motivated to avoid pain is a very powerful driver to start the change process, the motivation stops as soon as you've moved away from this pain.

It's essential to not just be moving away from something, but to also be certain about what you're moving towards instead. Therefore, it's crucial to not just focus on what you don't want, but to be crystal clear about what you do want to happen instead.

If you're waiting passively for your life to magically improve because you believe you somehow deserve it, you'll be waiting for the rest of your life while everyone else climbs all over you. In the face of setbacks, misfortune, pain and disappointment, there are only two questions powerful enough to get you out of bed in the morning to take your place in the race of life.

1. What do you really want?

2. What are you prepared to do about it?

Without a compelling vision for your life, the journey of overcoming insecurity gets way too hard, very quickly.

Practice 4 is all about letting the deep desires of your heart come to the surface again so you're clear about the future you're creating for yourself.

354
Let Go of the Illusion it Could've Been Different

I've run Townsville Marathon six times over the last 12 years. Every time I've dreamed of winning and trained intensely to achieve that dream. Yet, I've never even made the podium.

Amazingly, almost without exception, each year I show up, so do a bunch of super-fast runners, while each year I stay home, the winning time is always slower than my personal best. Historically, this has led to a bunch of wasted energy thinking about what could have happened if only I'd raced the opposite year!

It's very common to look back over past failures and disappointments and feel you could have, or should have, done better. Yet the fact that things could have been different is actually an illusion. It's never true. If you could have done it better, you actually would have. Your results were determined by everything that was happening for you and others in that moment.

Letting go of the illusion it could have been different frees you from abstract self-judgement and disappointment.

The only value in looking back, therefore, is to understand exactly what happened and why it happened so you're able to make better choices for your current and future decisions.

Practice 5 – Get Help from Someone Who Doesn't Care About You

As you embark on the journey of change and self-discovery, there comes a point where you're definitely going to need some help. Practice 5 is to realise that the hero always needs a guide. The challenge is finding the right one.

To change effectively, you have to be positioned as the adult. Lasting change requires internal motivation, not external encouragement. This means it's essential to enlist the help of someone in your life who does not care about you and has no vested interest in your results.

Their role is to simply treat you like a responsible adult. To position you as the one who created this mess and the only one with the power to get out of the mess, and then to serve you to get more of what you want.

Something remarkable becomes possible when you get help from someone who doesn't care about you. It means you can fully come out of hiding and be absolutely honest about what's going on in your life. It's the fear of judgement that keeps us pretending things are other than they really are.

To solve the insecurity problem, you'll need a high level of objectivity to get you out of story and into process. This can only be genuinely facilitated by someone with no agenda, other than to serve you, to get you more of what you want.

344
Practice 6 – Be the Hero

Because insecurity is a problem that exists within your own opinion of yourself, only you can solve this problem. Sooner or later, you have to face the thing you fear most about yourself and discover, once and for all, if it's actually true.

Everyone else knows you've always been enough and always will be, and that your fear is only smoke and mirrors, but your job is to discover this for yourself. If all you needed was someone else to say you're awesome, a few Instagram memes would have already done the trick.

At this point in the journey, the guide is no longer there and the hero must go on alone. Being the hero in your own life means you're eventually going to have to go fight the monster. That's what the hero does.

Specifically, Practice 6 is all about deconstructing the story you've been living out of all the way back to the start. This means examining the origins of your limiting beliefs and the very first time you decided you weren't enough.

The only way to find out the truth for sure is to face your deepest insecurity head on. This means you'll either die or come out the other side reborn, having dismantled the fear for good. That's when you're able to truly bring your gift to the world, unhindered by doubt, fear and self-limiting beliefs.

345
Practice 7 – Rewrite the Story

Practice 6 is all about completely deconstructing previously held beliefs about yourself until they no longer make sense and you're convinced they're simply not true. This cleans the slate for you to write a new and improved story. The final practice is to embrace your role as the script writer and design the story the way you'd like it to be, rather than living out of the story you created as a child.

The temptation is always to rush to Practice 7 and simply try to override the old opinions with positive affirmations. Yet until the old stories have been dismantled all the way back to the start, the prevailing negative narratives will continue to take over the moment you get tired, stressed or anxious.

Your current day results are merely the manifestation of what has already been created, either by design or default, in your mind. Therefore, if you want new results to show up in the real world, you have to go create them first.

Holding yourself accountable as the storyteller with 100% choice and responsibility is the key to experiencing lasting change in your life. As the victim of someone else's story, you have no power to change anything, but as the storyteller, you're the one with the pen, you're the one writing the scripts, and you're the one with all the power., so use it well!

346
Mistake 1 – Running Away from the Fear

....

Just as there are seven essential practices for overcoming insecurity, there are also seven big mistakes people make that exacerbate the insecurity problem.

The first big mistake people make when dealing with insecurity is to run away from the things they fear. This strategy comes from the faulty assumption that insecurity can never be removed from your life, so the best you can do is manage it instead. It seems that everything in the world is out to make you more insecure. You've just got to keep running and fill your life with so many things you don't even have time to think about what you're afraid of so that it doesn't catch up with you.

It's not that hard to guess this strategy is not very effective. Wherever you go, there you are. You can't escape yourself. When you lay your head down to sleep at night, there you are with your fears, and your fears taunt you.

What's more, every time you run, you teach yourself you don't have what it takes to deal with life and therefore end up undermining your self-esteem even further.

347
Mistake 2 – Hoping to be Rescued

The second biggest mistake people make when trying to deal with insecurity is hoping to be rescued. A central part of this mistake is a self-esteem strategy that looks to others to make them feel good.

Often people feel the reason they're insecure is because of the terrible, mean and hurtful things that have been said and done to them over the years. They hope they can find nice, kind, generous people instead to undo that bad work and make them feel like they're a good person. They seek people to rescue and validate them in order to be safe and feel ok about their life.

This mistake comes from a lack of understanding about where insecurity comes from in the first place. If you believe that other people created the problem, then you'll also look for other people to fix it.

This victim mentality leaves you powerless, waiting desperately for people to finally treat you like you deserve, and fix the pain of being hurt.

The problem is that if other people's kind words could actually make you feel good about yourself long term, you'd already have sorted the issue. The truth is that insecurity wasn't created by those around you. It was you who first decided you were no good, and therefore only you who can decide otherwise.

348
Mistake 3 – Using Pain Against Yourself

The third biggest mistake in dealing with insecurity is to use pain against yourself.

This mistake focuses on a strategy to mask, medicate and suppress pain. Just because something is bad for us, or is even killing us, doesn't mean we have to pay attention to that pain. Smoking is a classic example of this.

Pain doesn't feel good. We don't like pain and we don't know what to do with pain and so the plan is to do whatever is going to make you feel good now, in the moment, so you don't have to deal with this pain. Yet while it's possible to escape pain in the short term, the long-term pain continues to compound and escalate.

This mistake is the result of focusing entirely on the pain of change and ignoring the pain of staying the same. This means you end up using pain against yourself as every cell in your body resists forward progress because of the pain you've linked to it.

People struggle to quit smoking because they link pain to how hard it will be to change, while ignoring the pain of continuing as is. People remain in their insecurity for the same reason. It just feels too painful and costly to deal with. All the while, they've completely ignored the pain and cost of not dealing with it.

Mistake 4 – Dreaming in the Dark

....

The fourth biggest mistake in trying to overcome insecurity is dreaming in the dark.

When I ask people about the dream they have for their life, they often respond with vague, unexciting and poorly formed ideas that actually give them no motivation. Because they haven't found a way out of insecurity, their dreams are coloured by that fear.

It's as though they're dreaming in a dark room. They've been in darkness for so long they forgot what the sun looks like. Therefore, their dreams are so watered down and insipid they have no power to draw them forward. They're not compelling. The dreams are simply not powerful enough to cause them to be motivated to get out of their current situation and find a better way.

The trap when thinking about their life is to approach the question of what you really want from the viewpoint of your current level of pain, disappointment and fear.

If you never step outside of your current reality and fully allow yourself to see a picture of a brighter future, you'll lack the internal drive to do the deep soul work in order to free yourself from the prison you've created.

350
Mistake 5 – Getting Help from the Wrong People

The fifth biggest mistake in trying to overcome insecurity is people trying to solve insecurity look for help from the wrong people.

Typically, people look to friends and family, or even pay professionals to help sort their lives out. The problem is that, often, these helpers have a vested interest in you changing, which causes them to inadvertently disrupt the change process.

If you share a point of pain with someone who cares about you, or who needs you to do something, they cannot help but speak to you out of this agenda. They want you to be happy and healthy and not in pain, so the conversation quickly turns to advice and action.

As well-intentioned as this may be, it's never helpful. At best, it produces a short-term effort in the right direction, but inevitably positions them as the expert in your life, which creates resentment and actually disempowers you.

In every hero's journey, there's a wisdom character who prepares the hero to face the ultimate battle, yet they're not the hero in the story. The great challenge for those in the counselling, coaching or psychology space is not to confuse the world about who the hero is.

351
Mistake 6 – Fighting the Wrong Battle

The sixth biggest mistake in trying to overcome insecurity is fighting the wrong battle.

The process of dealing with insecurity really is the hero's journey. This means the central theme is the hero moving ever closer to the ultimate battle over the thing they're most afraid of.

The key mistake here is to think this battle is won by forcing yourself to do what you don't want to do. To feel the fear and act anyway is the popular slogan for this very mistake.

The wrong thinking is that part of you is afraid of not being good enough and you just need to defeat that part through the strength of your will.

This mistake turns to the old self-discipline strategy as the solution to every problem. Just be better, stronger and bigger! Just believe! To be the hero you just have to man up and get it done.

The true battle is to fight against the insecurity itself, not fight against the part of you that's insecure. Insecurity is never overcome by fighting against yourself. That's the wrong battle.

When you fight yourself, you only make the situation worse and further embed the belief that there's something deeply wrong with you.

352
Mistake 7 – Rushing to the End Too Soon

The final mistake in trying to solve the insecurity problem is perhaps the most common.

The personal development industry actually helps people make this mistake all the time. When people understand that change comes as they rewrite their story, the tendency is to want to go straight to Practice 7 and write a new story over the top of the old one.

The challenge is that if you don't deconstruct the old story first, then the moment you get tired, stressed or triggered, the old prevailing narrative takes over as per usual.

There's no quick fix, so just focusing on trying to be positive and writing loving affirmations on your mirror each morning isn't going to be enough to create lasting change. This is still merely a form of behaviour management.

As *Atomic Habits* author, James Clear, says: 'Changed behaviour is the evidence of a changed identity. You can't create a new identity while the old one is still in operation.'

In order to rewrite the story you're living out of, you need to clear the slate first.

353
Self-sabotage

Self-sabotage is entirely an issue of lack of self-permission.

When your subconscious perceives more danger, risk or potential loss in your desired change than where you're currently positioned, it will sabotage your plans. You clearly don't have permission to move forward.

Rather than getting frustrated and annoyed with yourself, the key is to understand the positive intention of this sabotage and to see it as a form of protection. This allows you to have a conversation with yourself to see what conditions would need to be satisfied before you could move forward unhindered.

One of the most important discoveries of your life is that fighting against yourself is a young person's strategy. If you don't have your own permission to succeed, forcing harder only results in the internal handbrake being reefed on harder as well. You'll never win that battle. Ending the war and making peace with yourself is perhaps the most important work of your life.

Imagine what would be possible once you're able to work with yourself rather than being positioned as your own worst enemy.

355
Gratitude – Progress – Optimism

Glen Carlson[91] from Dent Global has shown me that one of the key patterns of successful entrepreneurs is that they start their day and their meetings with gratitude, progress and optimism.

These three questions help them orient themselves this way:

1. What am I incredibly grateful for in my life right now?

2. What wins, big or small, can I notice and celebrate as evidence of real progress?

3. What am I optimistic about for the future and what projects, ideas, plans or goals am I excited about?

With our inbuilt negativity bias, it's still so much easier to focus on lack, failure and disappointment by asking a very different set of questions instead:

1. What's not right?

2. What's missing?

3. What haven't I done well?

One path leads to life and growth, the other to death and decay. The cool thing is that focus is not chosen for us, it's one of the wonderful things we get to decide about every day.

This simple shift in focus, and therefore the quality of the questions you're asking yourself, have massive power to change almost every area of your life.

356
The Sunk Cost Bias

....

Have you ever overeaten at a buffet, worn shoes too small for you, finished a book you don't like or stayed friends with someone who is toxic? This is all due to a fantastic piece of psychology called the sunk cost bias.[92]

We think we make rational decisions based on the future value of objects, investments and experiences. The truth, however, is our decisions are tainted by the emotional investments we accumulate, and the more you invest in something, the harder it becomes to abandon it.

The cost is 'sunk' because it was a one-time expense and cannot be recovered once spent.

Once you're full, you don't get more value by eating more food because you've already spent your money. You can't take the shoes back now you've worn them, and you don't get any extra value by rubbing the skin off the end of your toes. The book you're not enjoying is now robbing you of time you could be spending elsewhere and ending a friendship now doesn't devalue the good times you shared in the past.

The two keys to avoid this bias are:

1. Be aware that your brain will try to convince you to stick with your investments.

2. Ask yourself if you were able to make a fresh choice now, would you still choose this?

Avoiding the sunk cost bias is essential to moving forward and choosing the things that are best for you.

357
Having a Clear Rationale

Have you considered the importance of having a clear rationale for every area of your life? Are you sure about what you're doing and, more importantly, why you're doing it?

Perhaps you had a clear rationale once upon a time but if you're honest, that no longer makes any sense in this season of life. Or maybe you've never had a rationale at all. You're just doing what you do because you fell into it, someone suggested you should do it, or there were no other available options.

Often people are afraid that having an opinion means others can judge or ridicule you, yet the most attractive people in life are always those who know exactly what they want.

Having a clear rationale for the key areas of your life forms some of your most important adult thinking. There are a thousand opinions about what is right or wrong. Who really knows which one is best? The point is, if you're not setting the rules of engagement, something, or someone else, will set them for you.

Get in the game by having a clear plan. It doesn't have to be your rationale forever but being where you are on purpose gives you a sense of agency over what your life looks like right now and how it will be in the future.

358
Moving from the Known to the Unknown

One of the most powerful problem-solving techniques I've developed over the course of my life is to move from the known to the unknown.

Most people do the opposite and start with what they don't know instead. Yet beginning with the unknown inevitably leads to becoming overwhelmed and confused. This is to dive into the hardest part of the problem first. It proves impossible to navigate your way forward simply because of the vast amount of stuff you don't know!

However, when you start with what you do know and what you're sure about, and then move towards what you don't know from this position of certainty, you drastically narrow the field of possibilities to only a few variables. This also allows you to come at the problem with the confidence it can be solved.

As soon as you remind yourself about what you already know to be true, you get very clear about what the answer isn't. This often only leaves two or three possible solutions to test and discover. Problem solving then becomes a process of elimination from a place of confidence.

While this process still may not expose all the unknowns, it gives you all the clarity you need to take the correct next step and work out the rest from there.

359
Abundance vs Scarcity

Both abundance and scarcity are all around us every day. Which one you predominately experience more of is entirely up to you.

Every moment, we have the capacity to reach into the extraordinary abundance of life, or shrivel up in the wasteland of scarcity, simply by what we're paying attention to.

For example, if you remove entitlement and expectation for what should be, you're left with gratitude for what is. This allows you to understand the grace that's been afforded to you to even be here right now, alive, full of choice and opportunity.

From there, it's clear to also see we each have an abundant amount of opportunity, time, energy, creativity and possibility in every moment, and that this is always true whether we can see it or not. There's beauty in everything, and nothing is empty or devoid of value.

One of the most profound and powerful shifts to move towards wealth is to realise that you're already incredibly wealthy! No matter who you are or what you do or do not have, if you're alive, you have access to life. That is a place of abundance.

Abundance or scarcity really is your choice.

360
Worrying About the Future

Anxiety is often part of an unresourceful strategy to meet our need for certainty. When things that concern us feel out of our control, investing energy into worrying about them is a subconscious attempt to somehow gain a measure of control over the outcome or contribute positively to these events.

However, as Baz Luhrmann's song goes: '

Worrying about the future is as effective as trying to solve an algebra equation by chewing bubble gum. The real troubles in your life will always be the things that never crossed your worried mind. [93]

When someone sees you worrying unnecessarily and tells you to settle down, it's always super annoying, but the point is they're right. Being stressed, anxious and wound up like a cog is not helping you solve the challenges you're facing, nor is it adding any value to your overall health and wellbeing.

Developing rituals and practices that allow you to stop, breathe and return to a state of calm when you feel anxious, is one of the most powerful and kind intentions you can make towards your own success and growth. This then allows you to focus only on what you can control. Instead of looking for certainty in the event to work out the way you want, you find certainty in your ability to deal with the event however it works out.

In the words of Jesus: 'Therefore, do not worry about tomorrow, for tomorrow will worry about itself. Each day has enough trouble of its own.'[94]

361
Live as Though Your Father Is Dead

Father of modern psychotherapy, Sigmund Freud, observed that a human's greatest challenge was to break free from the nest. He taught that there were great forces at play working against this freedom, both in the parent and in the child, but that ultimately all dysfunction in life came through this tendency to get stuck within the family bounds.[95]

In reference to Freud's idea, David Deida says a man should therefore live as though his father is dead. That is, a man must love his father and yet be free of his father's expectations and criticisms in order to be a free man.

Deida says:

How would you have lived your life differently if you had never tried to please your father? If you never tried to show your father that you were worthy? If you never felt burdened by your father's critical eye? For the next three days, do at least one activity a day that you have avoided or suppressed because of the influence of your father. In this way, practise being free of his subtle expectations, which may now reside within your own self-judgement. Practise being free in this way, once each day for three days, even if you still feel fearful, limited, unworthy or burdened by your father's expectations.[96]

This is in no way designed to undermine your relationship with your father or to be ungrateful for his contribution to your life. It's simply to understand your need to stand on his shoulders and grow beyond his life as you live your own.

362
Assertiveness is Fruit

Learning to say, 'I'm sorry, that doesn't work for me,' is something we all kind of realise is an important part of being an adult. But why is assertiveness so hard in the real world?

Contrary to popular opinion, assertiveness is not a skill to learn, but a fruit to develop. It turns out that true assertiveness is simply the fruit of dealing with your neediness by taking full ownership of your own value and worth.

Assertiveness without letting go of neediness is actually very dangerous. It leaves you vulnerable to coming off second best. If you confront or stand up to those you need something from, they have the direct power to hurt you by withholding what you need.

However, if you're comfortable in your own skin and don't need external validation to feel good about yourself, you naturally become assertive. As a result of this internal ownership, confident words and actions flow naturally without aggression, defensiveness or even trying to deliberately create healthy boundaries.

There really is no one in your world who can get away with treating you poorly. It simply doesn't make sense! You don't need anything from them, so why tolerate what is less than you desire or deserve?

If you want to be more assertive, you have to be less needy first.

363
Gaslighting

Have you ever been gaslighted? Have you ever gaslighted someone else? Perhaps you have never understood what this term even means.

1. Gaslighting is a form of psychological manipulation where a person makes someone else question their own memory, judgement or perception of reality. This often creates cognitive dissonance and massively undermines their self-esteem.[97]

2. Gaslighting happens when the status of a relationship changes due to an issue being raised, a problem addressed or holding the person to account for a mistake they've made.

3. This causes the person to feel threatened, insecure and backed into a corner. Therefore, they must defend their vulnerability and fight for control. They then manipulate the data by withholding info, trivialising, denying, counterattacking, questioning and sowing seeds of doubt.

4. Here are five keys to avoid and overcome the gaslighting trap:

5. Rather than looking to strong people in your life to set direction for you, find your true north internally. Be clear about what is true for you.

6. Develop your capacity to self-reference. When your sanity is being questioned or undermined, it's essential to be your own safety and have your own back.

7. Don't cling to relationships. Allow people to flow in and out of your life as the seasons dictate.

8. Deal with your own insecurity first. Take the plank out of your own eye to be able to see clearly to remove the speck from your brother's eye.[98]

9. Take nothing personally. Remember, it's not about you.[99]

364
Deep Change

When you get notifications on your phone to download and install the latest operating system updates, how do you respond?

However inconvenient these updates may be, if you don't get them your system becomes incompatible with your apps and they eventually stop working all together.

Interestingly, this is similar to how many people deal with their own internal operating systems. The initial set-up was so long ago it has no capacity to deal with the complexity of modern life.

What if improving the quality of your life was entirely dependent on downloading and installing these five key updates to your internal operating system?[100]

1. Fully becoming an adult instead of meeting your needs as a child.

2. Using self-permission as motivation instead of self-discipline.

3. Problem-solving by addressing the core issues rather than dealing with the surface symptoms.

4. Processing new challenges by facing up to life instead of running away.

5. Positioning yourself as the storyteller of your own narrative rather than seeing yourself as the actor in a story written by someone else.

Genuine and lasting improvement becomes inevitable when you make all five upgrades to your internal operating systems.

365
Subtracting

I could think of no better way to wrap up 365 segments than with this wisdom from one of my favourite authors.

Derek Sivers says that life can be improved by adding, or by subtracting. The world pushes us to add because that benefits the world. But the secret is to focus on subtracting. [101]

The adding mindset is deeply ingrained and therefore it's far easier to think we need something else that's missing rather than instead looking at what to remove.

The least successful people I know run in conflicting directions, are drawn to distractions, say yes to almost everything and are chained to emotional obstacles.

The most successful people I know have a narrow focus, protect themselves against time wasters, say no to almost everything and have let go of old limiting beliefs.

More people die from eating too much than from eating too little. Most of us have too much baggage, too many commitments and too many priorities.

Subtracting reminds us we already have everything we need inside us. Success comes as we remove the things that are in the way.

TOPIC INDEX

Abundance 283, 359.
Accountability 91, 132.
Adulting 316, 320.
Advice 144, 220, 350.
Anxiety 152, 291, 360.
Apologizing 222, 233, 276.
Assertiveness 362.
Awareness 56, 66, 91, 197.
Bad days 72, 141, 277.
Beauty 75.
Be-Do-Have 34.
Behaviour Management 19, 41.
Beliefs 46, 197, 211, 234, 250.
Blame 2, 4, 217, 298, 306.
Busyness 50, 184, 263, 304.
Certainty 38, 116, 225, 235, 305, 360.
Choice 1, 18, 52, 73, 197, 205.
Chunk Size 30, 102.
Comparison 89, 113, 216, 302.
Complaining 3, 251.
Confidence 43, 152, 253.
Conflict 62, 64, 138, 147, 222.
Consequence 10, 266.
Consistency 70, 72.
Contribution 163, 169.
Control 12, 95, 116, 360.

Core Issues 226
Courage 160, 253.
Decisions 110, 223, 256.
De-Cluttering 172.
Depression 224.
Desire 7, 94, 156, 219.
Disappointment 88, 278, 321.
Doubt 46, 232, 238.
Dreams 151, 183, 349.
Dress 86, 330.
Ego 66, 162.
Emotions 70, 76, 171, 262.
Energy Management 11, 105, 114, 128, 179.
Entrepreneurship 168, 246, 355.
Evidence 17, 46.
Excuse 2, 217.
Exercise 36, 74, 106.
Expectations 71, 145, 190, 278, 361.
Experience 5, 14, 49, 58, 318, 336.
Failure 29, 154, 277, 295.
Fear 69, 115-119, 256, 262, 304, 338, 346.
Fighting Yourself 32, 63, 205-207, 351, 353.
Flow 152, 184, 311.
Focus 13, 15, 44, 61, 76, 179, 355.
Forgiveness 96
Freedom 87, 319.
Friendships 146, 275.

Frustration 53, 72, 307.
Gaslighting 363.
Generosity 121.
Goals 8, 60, 101, 115, 193, 266.
Grace 210.
Gratitude 173, 355.
Growth 170, 189, 202, 259.
Guarantees 225.
Happiness 78, 141, 258, 267, 284.
Hastiness 49.
Health 74, 106, 141, 161, 243, 327.
Hero 126, 344, 350-351.
Honesty 98, 155.
Honour 269, 289.
Hope 1, 124, 273, 347.
Humility 84
Hurt 47, 96, 99.
Illusions 195.
Imagination 62, 87.
Influence 24, 95, 144.
Insecurity 243, 249, 339-352.
Intention 10, 20, 266, 332.
Joy 157.
Judgment 29, 67, 244.
Karpman Drama Triangle 180.
Keeping Track 252.
Knowledge 174, 200.

367

Labels 97.
Language 14, 18, 83, 112, 142.
Laziness 114, 304.
Learning 109, 202.
Limiting Beliefs 250, 318.
Loneliness 181.
Love 88, 99, 202, 262, 329.
Lying 155, 200.
Madness 228, 251.
Manipulation 24, 363.
Meds 327.
Men 271.
Metaphors 142.
Mind 56, 148, 204.
Mistakes 212, 346-352.
Momentum 23
Money 22, 216, 246.
Multitasking 187.
Narcissism 137, 280.
Negotiability 68.
Nuance 133.
Nutrition 106.
Observer 65.
One-Minute Manager 313.
Optimism 295, 355.
Outcome 8, 10, 12, 61, 193.
Overthinking 131.
Pain 28, 32, 308, 341, 348.
Parents 100, 123, 178, 264.
Parkinson's Law 153.
Partner 329.
Peace 138, 199, 254.

Peak Performance 33, 193.
Perception 48.
Perfectionism 33.
Persecutor 180, 335.
Pessimism 294.
Physiology 16.
Pleasure 28, 39.
Possibilities 274.
Power 2, 182, 210.
Pressure 282.
Presupposition 286, 287.
Pretending 148, 200.
Priorities 26.
Prize 57, 122.
Problem Solving 333.
Productivity 187, 229.
Progress 23, 355.
Purpose 201, 315.
Questions 7, 25, 59, 325, 333, 334, 355.
Readiness 81, 219.
Rebellion 166.
Reframe 42, 58.
Relationships 4, 57, 64, 71, 99, 107, 122, 134, 146, 177, 209, 247, 275, 329.
Relaxation 261.
Resistance 198
Responsibility 298, 306, 340.
Rest 55, 105, 128, 184, 255, 263.
Review 331, 334.
Reward 3, 39.
Rituals 36, 108, 133.
Romance 122, 177.
Rules 40, 209.

Run Away 27, 346.
Safety 38, 42, 118, 188.
Scarcity 359.
Self-Acceptance 190.
Self-Deception 314.
Self-Doubt 232.
Self-Permission 289, 353.
Self-Protection 9, 206.
Self-Sabotage 206, 207, 353.
Self-Talk 35.
Setbacks 278, 303.
Settling 241, 242.
Shame 272.
Shiny Object Syndrome 143.
Significance 129, 218, 301.
Six Core Needs 19, 92.
Social Skills 86.
Sorry 124, 233, 362.
Spiral Dynamics 163-169.
Stakeholders 104.
State 12-16, 108, 117, 133, 152, 214, 268.
Story 6, 91, 136, 223, 268, 291, 318, 345, 352.
Strategy 268
Stress 127.
Submitting 192.
Subtracting 365.
Success 77, 115-119, 130, 159, 237, 290.
Suffering 309.
Surrender 285.
Survival 164.
System 167, 364.

Thoughts 56, 66, 204, 310, 328.
Time Management 11, 92.
Transformation 91.
Tribe 165.
Trust 134, 222.
Validation 301.
Values 20, 40.
Victim 2, 34, 180, 213, 287, 298, 335.
Visualisation 85.
Vulnerability 134, 288.
Wanting 67.
Why 25.
Willpower 21, 31.
Winning 90, 102, 208.
Wisdom 326.
Wish 101, 266.
Women 270
Worry 360.
Worth 145, 172, 301.
Wrong 276, 279, 350, 351.
Yes 203, 235, 296, 331.

Endnotes

1. "With great power there must also come great responsibility", or simply "With great power comes great responsibility", alternatively known as the Peter Parker principle, is a proverb popularised by the Spider-Man comic books written by Stan Lee. The quote is used in politics and monarchy, in law enforcement and public safety, by journalists and book authors, and in various media and memes.
2. Dr Phil McGraw https://en.wikipedia.org/wiki/Phil_McGraw
3. This model was developed by John Grinder as a key part of new code NLP. In classical code NLP, the person will ask the client for the outcome that they are seeking, what is called a well-formed outcome. With New Code NLP, Grinder claims that when the person gives a conscious answer there is also an unconscious component, a part, that may not necessarily agree with the conscious outcome.

   Essentially, he says that if the conscious mind could get the desired outcome, it would have already done so. So, in NEW CODE NLP they calibrate both the conscious and unconscious responses to the well-formed outcome to make sure that they are in agreement. If the conscious outcome and the unconscious are not in alignment. it is the job of the practitioner to first get them in agreement before doing the intervention.

   Grinder claims that when he and Richard worked with clients they did this aligning but in the classical model of NLP this aspect is not stressed. So, with his NEW CODE NLP this was what he sought to develop and teach.

   The six steps reframe is similar to what John seems to be talking about. It is a content free process that seeks to get all of the parts in alignment and working toward the same goal before asking the unconscious to accept the intervention. In NLP terms this is called the ecology of the system, and it implies that making any change may have far and long reaching other affects in other aspects of the clients life than just the desired change, and are these other changes desirable? https://www.mastersamnaples-nlp-hypnotherapy.com/JohnGrinder.html
4. https://www.tonyrobbins.com/mind-meaning/do-you-need-to-feel-significant/
5. John Maxwell. The 21 irrefutable laws of leadership. Law 2 — The law of influence
6. https://www.time-management-techniques.com/tony-robbins-chunking.html
7. https://seths.blog/2011/03/reject-the-tyranny-of-being-picked-pick-yourself/
8. Charlie Wilson's War is a 2007 American biographical comedy-drama film, based on the story of U.S. Congressman Charlie Wilson and CIA operative Gust Avrakotos, whose efforts led to Operation Cyclone, a program to organize and support the Afghan mujahideen during the Soviet–Afghan War.
9. This quote is from: Awaken the Giant Within: How to Take Immediate Control of Your Mental, Emotional, Physical and Financial Destiny!
10. https://en.wikipedia.org/wiki/Nick_Vujicic Nick describes his life story in his first book "Life without limits" describes his life story.
11. First developed by George T. Doran. https://en.wikipedia.org/wiki/SMART_criteria
12. Adapted from the NLP technique called perceptual positions. https://www.nlp-techniques.org/what-is-nlp/perceptual-positions/

13 The full quote from "The power of now" by Eckart Tolle. Ego is the unobserved mind that runs your life when you are not present as the witnessing consciousness, the watcher. The ego perceives itself as a separate fragment in a hostile universe, with no real inner connection to any other being, surrounded by other egos which it either sees as a potential threat or which it will attempt to use for its own ends. The basic ego patterns are designed to combat its own deep-seated fear and sense of lack. They are resistance, control, power, greed, defence, attack. Some of the ego's strategies are extremely clever, yet they never truly solve any of its problems, simply because the ego itself is the problem.

14 The Wizard of Oz is a 1939 American musical nightmare fantasy film produced by Metro-Goldwyn-Mayer.

15 "The conflict between who we are and who we want to be is at the core of the human struggle. Duality, in fact, lies at the very center of the human experience. Life and death, good and evil, hope and resignation coexist in every person and exert their force in every facet of our lives. If we know courage, it is because we have also experienced fear; if we can recognize honesty, it is because we have encountered deceit. And yet most of us deny or ignore our dualistic nature."
– Deepak Chopra, The Shadow Effect: Illuminating the Hidden Power of Your True Self

16 "Don't seek happiness. If you seek it, you won't find it, because seeking is the antithesis of happiness. Happiness is ever elusive, but freedom from unhappiness is attainable now, by facing what is rather than making up stories about it."
Eckhart Tolle (2008). "Oneness with All Life: Inspirational Selections from A New Earth", p.12, Penguin

17 All things are created twice either by design or by default. Stephen Covey, 'The seven habits of highly effective people' p 100.

18 https://www.marcandangel.com

19 Marianne Williamson, A Return to Love: Reflections on the Principles of "A Course in Miracles"

20 Here is the full quote attributed to him. "Imagination is more important than knowledge. For knowledge is limited to all we now know and understand, while imagination embraces the entire world, and all there ever will be to know and understand."

21 https://en.wikipedia.org/wiki/Shadowlands_(1993_film)

22 C.S. Lewis, The Four Loves, 1960

23 The full quote is from the stanza found in his poem Canto 27.
I hold it true, whate'er befall.
I feel it when I sorrow most.
Tis better to have loved and lost
Than never to have loved at all.
Alfred, Lord Tennyson.

24 Adapted from The 4 A's model developed by Brian Grasso and Carrie Campbell. http://www.brianandcarrie.live

25 https://www.amazon.com.au/Breaking-Habit-Being-Yourself-Create/dp/1401938094

26 Proverbs 13:12

27 Adapted from Steven Covey. 7 Habits of highly effective people. pp.81-94 Covey introduced the idea as two circles only. The circle of concern and the circle of influence
28 The Simpsons. Season 5 Episode 6
29 https://www.linkedin.com/in/matt-waldron-7146811a/
30 In 1949, Joseph Campbell summarised all the most loved stories, myths and fables throughout history and noticed they followed a similar pattern, which he called *The Hero's Journey*. It is also an amazing metaphor for doing life well.
31 https://en.wikipedia.org/wiki/Conservation_of_energy
32 This idea comes from Tony Robbins. Here is the full quote from page 26 of his book *Unlimited power* "Long ago, I realized that success leaves clues, and that people who produce outstanding results do specific things to create those results...I believed that if I precisely duplicated the actions of others, I could reproduce the same quality of results that they had."
33 https://www.amazon.com.au/Five-Dysfunctions-Team-Leadership-Fable/dp/0787960756
34 Brian McLaren explains the power of the word 'This' (page 76) as part of his chapter section on 'Thanks' in his book *Naked Spirituality*
35 https://www.amazon.com.au/Switch-Chip-Heath/dp/0385528752
36 https://www.forbes.com/sites/danschawbel/2013/01/03/daniel-pink-says-that-in-todays-world-were-all-salespeople/#1ca08d013818
37 https://en.wikipedia.org/wiki/Parkinson%27s_law
38 Sir Ken Robinson. TED talk — Do schools kill creativity? https://www.youtube.com/watch?v=iG9CE55wbtY&feature=emb_title
39 Siimon Reynolds. *Why people fail. The 16 obstacles to success and how you can overcome them.* Introduction, P.XI
40 Pixie Turner. The No Need To Diet Book: Become a Diet Rebel and Make Friends with Food

By Pixie Turner

"Not only does it make us feel mentally miserable, it also increases the stress hormone Cortisol, which makes you feel physically crap on top of that and potentially makes those cravings worse"
41 https://www.amazon.com.au/Spiral-Dynamics-Mastering-Values-Leadership/dp/1405133562
42 https://en.wikipedia.org/wiki/Clare_W._Graves
43 https://www.goodreads.com/quotes/7196256-gratitude-in-advance-is-the-most-powerful-creative-force-in
44 https://en.wikipedia.org/wiki/Curse_of_knowledge
45 https://en.wikipedia.org/wiki/Karpman_drama_triangle
46 https://futurism.com/the-physics-of-death
47 https://en.wikipedia.org/wiki/Helen_Keller
48 https://copyblogger.com/robert-greene-mastery/
49 https://www.5lovelanguages.com
50 https://www.amazon.com.au/You-Are-Not-Your-Brain-ebook/dp/B004XFYRMA

51. This idea was taken from Seth's daily blog: https://Seths.blog
52. Matthew 25:14-30
53. Matthew 9:14-17
54. https://boxofcrayons.com/the-coaching-habit-book/
55. Jim Carrey's Inspiring Commencement Speech Maharishi University. 2014 https://youtu.be/q2rVDCrt6QY
56. https://robbell.com
57. https://www.goodreads.com/quotes/7663035-the-quality-of-your-life-is-a-direct-reflection-of
58. Eckhart Tolle: A new earth pp.11-12
59. https://www.ted.com/talks/alan_iny_reigniting_creativity_in_business
60. Here is his full quote on this subject: "Making a true decision, unlike saying, "I'd like to quit smoking," is cutting off any other possibility. In fact, the word "decision" comes from the Latin roots de, which means "from," and caedere, which means "to cut." Making a true decision means committing to achieving a result, and then cutting yourself off from any other possibility. When you truly decide you'll never smoke cigarettes again, that's it. It's over! You no longer even consider the possibility of smoking." – Anthony Robbins, Awaken the Giant Within: How to Take Immediate Control of Your Mental, Emotional, Physical and Financial Destiny!
61. https://www.youtube.com/watch?v=U9eiHUPbtJE
62. http://www.gregorygeorgeconsulting.com
63. https://fourhourworkweek.com
64. Eckhart Tolle, The Power of Now: A Guide to Spiritual Enlightenment
65. https://tim.blog/2018/06/05/the-tim-ferriss-show-transcripts-seth-godin-on-how-to-think-small-to-go-big/
66. Tim Ferriss. The 4 hour work week.
67. Here is the full quote: "There are only two emotions: love and fear. All positive emotions come from love, all negative emotions from fear. From love flows happiness, contentment, peace, and joy. From fear comes anger, hate, anxiety and guilt. It's true that there are only two primary emotions, love and fear. But it's more accurate to say that there is only love or fear, for we cannot feel these two emotions together, at exactly the same time. They're opposites. If we're in fear, we are not in a place of love. When we're in a place of love, we cannot be in a place of fear."
68. https://tim.blog/pavel-tsatsouline-on-the-tim-ferriss-show-transcript/
69. Mark Manson. The subtle art of not giving a f*ck
70. https://www.goodreads.com/quotes/97717-when-you-have-exhausted-all-possibilities-remember-this---you
71. https://en.wikipedia.org/wiki/Hero%27s_journey
72. Mark Manson. The subtle art of not giving a f*ck. P.134
73. https://www.goodreads.com/quotes/8800-the-illiterate-of-the-21st-century-will-not-be-those
74. From Martin Seligman's book Learned Optimism. https://en.wikipedia.org/wiki/Learned_optimism

75   Brenè Brown. 'The gifts of imperfection'. https://www.actionablebooks.com/en-ca/summaries/the-gifts-of-imperfection-2/
76   From my book Elegantly simple solutions to complex people problems. P 2
77   Mark Manson. The subtle art of not giving a f*ck.
78   Ibid. 69
79   Matthew 5:37
80   https://www.cnbc.com/2016/08/25/tim-ferriss-being-perpetually-busy-is-a-kind-of-laziness.html
81   Mark Manson — The subtle art of not giving a f*ck
82   Essentialism by Greg McKeown https://gregmckeown.com/book/
83   https://en.wikiquote.org/wiki/Richard_Feynman#The_Character_of_Physical_Law_(1965) "Cargo Cult Science", adapted from a 1974 Caltech commencement address; also published in *Surely You're Joking, Mr. Feynman!*, p. 343
84   Proverbs 4:7, 8:11, 16:16
85   Matthew 11:19
86   https://www.linkedin.com/in/ellenjacksonpotential/
87   Don Miguel Ruiz — The 4 Agreements.
88   Steven Kotler and Jamie Wheal quote Keegan in their book — Stealing fire. P38.
89   Here is the full quote from The 7 habits of highly effective people — "We are not our feelings. We are not our moods. We are not even our thoughts. The very fact that we can think about these things separates us from them and from the animal world. Self-awareness enables us to stand apart and examine even the way we "see" ourselves—our self-paradigm, the most fundamental paradigm of effectiveness. It affects not only our attitudes and behaviours, but also how we see other people."
90   The full framework for overcoming insecurity is in my book Unhindered — The seven essential practices for overcoming insecurity. www.unhinderedbook.com
91   https://www.linkedin.com/in/glencarlson/
92   https://en.wikipedia.org/wiki/Sunk_cost
93   From the Baz Luhrmann song, Everybody's free to wear sunscreen https://www.youtube.com/watch?v=5giWfpANMac
94   Matthew 6:34
95   Jordan Peterson brilliantly summarises the work of Freud this way. https://www.youtube.com/watch?v=PC8FNfMIIhg
96   David Deida — The way of the superior man. Chapter 3 — Live as though your father is dead. Page 19.
97   https://en.wikipedia.org/wiki/Gaslighting
98   Matthew 7:5
99   This is the second of the four agreements. Don Miguel Ruiz. The four agreements.
100 I cover these five upgrades in depth in my book — Unhindered. The seven essential practices for overcoming insecurity. www.unhinderebook.com
101 https://sive.rs/subtract